BREAKTHROUGH

BREAKTHROUGH

*How Great Companies Set Outrageous
Objectives and Achieve Them*

BILL DAVIDSON

JOHN WILEY & SONS, INC.

Published by John Wiley & Sons, Inc., Hoboken, New Jersey.
Published simultaneously in Canada.

For general information on our other products and services please contact our Customer Care
Department within the United States at (800) 762-2974, outside the United States at (317) 572-3993
or fax (317) 572-4002.

Wiley also publishes its books in a variety of electronic formats. Some content that appears in print
may not be available in electronic books. For more information about Wiley products, visit our web
site at *www.wiley.com*.

Library of Congress Cataloging-in-Publication Data

Davidson, William Harley, 1951–
    Breakthrough : how great companies set outrageous objectives, and achieve them / Bill Davidson.
        p. cm.
    Includes bibliographical references and index.
    ISBN 0-471-45440-0 (CLOTH)
    1. Organizational change. 2. Success in business. I. Title.
HD58.8.D366 2003
658.4′063—dc21

                                                                        2003010889

Printed in the United States of America.
10 9 8 7 6 5 4 3 2 1

CONTENTS

To Lisa,

bright and true,

and

Brad,

who lightens the journey

BREAKTHROUGH

CHAPTER 1

BREAKTHROUGH DYNAMICS

BREAKTHROUGH IS the bedrock of business success. Every corporate success cycle starts with an innovation that triggers superior performance. Aspiring firms everywhere seek to find breakthroughs that will focus their energy and fuel their success. Few find them, and not all that do are able to realize their full potential. For those fortunate few firms who find breakthroughs and fulfill their promise, life is glorious. However, cycles of superior performance that begin with breakthrough will inevitably end—unless further innovation occurs to renew the firm's position and performance. Today's leaders must ask themselves the following questions: "When will we need to begin our next breakthrough? What will it be?" Don't wait until the bitter end to start your next success cycle.

The transition from one success cycle to the next is never easy. The Buddhist term *bardo* refers to a period between phases of existence—a time that is pregnant with possibilities. These transition times offer many pathways and choices. The concept is particularly relevant in the life of corporations. It was in such a transition time that this book was born.

It all began in Ralph Waldo Emerson's library. In the fall of 1992, IBM's top 18 senior executives met for their annual strategy review at Emerson's estate in western Massachusetts. IBM had just completed an extraordinary decade. In the 1980s, it almost single-handedly reversed the tide of Japanese invasion of U.S. markets. In a bruising competition that was played on a grand stage of commercial, political, diplomatic, and legal fronts, the Japanese advance in high tech had largely been neutralized. As the 1990s began, IBM stood on top of the tallest peak in the global economy. Its recent history had been glorious. In 1990, it had reported a profit of $6 billion on $69 billion in revenue, making it the most profitable company in the world. At about $50 billion, IBM enjoyed the largest stock market capitalization in America at the end of 1990. The company had been recognized as the most admired corporation in the United States by *Fortune* as recently as 1986. All of these achievements would soon be forgotten.

As the senior team gathered in Emerson's library, fractures were beginning to appear in the foundation of IBM's empire. IBM's worldwide market share in computing had fallen from about 37 percent in 1983 to 23 percent in 1991.[1] Collapsing computer prices and steep declines in sales of its high-margin mainframes were hurting profits. Corporate customers were converting to increasingly powerful minicomputers and workstations, abandoning the handcuffs of IBM's proprietary mainframe systems for less expensive, more open systems that could use hardware from competing manufacturers.

The mainframe had been central to IBM's business model for decades, but Big Blue's problems were not driven by attachment to a mainframe mindset. It was playing hard in all segments of the computing market. Its AS400 minicomputers racked up $15 billion in sales in 1991, putting great pressure on number 2 hardware vendor DEC, who would not survive the decade. In the workstation market, the RS600 was a strong contender, and IBM had just slashed prices by 60 percent. Big Blue had made a quick, aggressive entry into the PC business—the only established computing firm to do so. This was not an arrogant incumbent ignoring new developments in its business.

Yet the feeling that Big Blue was losing control of its market was inescapable. In the PC arena, IBM protégés Intel and Microsoft were beginning to put their own stamp on the market. IBM had embraced these two key suppliers to support its rapid entry into the PC business, slamming the door on Japanese competitors in the low end of the computing market in the process. IBM had single-handedly "made" Microsoft when it selected DOS as the operating system for its PC. In 1983, IBM had purchased 12 percent of Intel, injecting some $250 million into the company in order to ensure its long-term survival in the face of severe Japanese pressure in the semiconductor business. IBM's ownership position eventually grew to 20 percent at a total purchase cost of $642 million. In 1987, IBM sold its Intel holdings of roughly 18 million shares for just over $1 billion. (In 2000, those Intel shares would have been worth over $66 billion.) Both companies owed their very existence to IBM. Now Intel and Microsoft were seeking to shape the PC market to their advantage and to capture the bulk of the profit stream from the main growth vector in computing.

While Intel and Microsoft's prospects looked strong, the latest financial projections for IBM were deeply disturbing. CEO John Akers, who called his team to order in the Ralph Waldo Emerson library, made two things clear: The company was poised on the brink of what seemed to be a bottomless financial disaster, and radical thinking was needed if the company was to avoid the impending train wreck.

In the Emerson library that day, the management team that had outperformed all others over the past decade struggled to recognize that their success cycle was coming to an end. Not all the attendees were prepared to accept this conclusion, but some spoke heatedly about the need for urgent action. Akers and others spoke with conviction about the need for a new formula. But this day was not to be about new strategies and new beginnings. It was a day to acknowledge that a glorious era had come to an end.

Within the quarter, IBM would announce the then-largest loss in corporate history, reporting almost a $5 billion charge for its first wave of workforce reductions. Notably, IBM reported an operating loss for the fourth quarter of 1992, the first in the company's 79-year history. Facing severe cash constraints, it also cut its dividend by more than 50 percent. The company's share price, recently as high as $175, collapsed to less than $50 per share. Aker's resignation came one week later, with the following statement: "It is the right time in IBM's business transformation to identify new leadership."

A transition period had begun. It was clear that IBM had to transform itself to survive, but the new path was uncertain. As part of that journey, IBM engaged our group, Management Education Services Associates (MESA) Research Group, to conduct in-depth studies of how other firms had achieved successful business transformation. That initial research project grew into a larger endeavor. Over the past decade we have observed, studied, and worked with seventy companies in various stages of business breakthrough and transformation, including IBM itself. We've learned a great deal from these breakthrough companies and their leaders. My goal in this book is to synthesize, sharpen, and share those learnings for use in your team's success cycle. It all begins with breakthrough.

THE ORIGINS OF BREAKTHROUGH

Think of breakthrough as enterprise-scale innovation—significant enough to shape an emerging enterprise or to reform the core of an existing organization. Breakthroughs can originate from "point" product or process innovations, but they ultimately evolve into an entirely new business model that delivers superior operating and profit performance, leading to both a new corporate profile and a new market position for the breakthrough company, as seen in Figure 1.1. A successful breakthrough fundamentally redefines the innovating firm—and in many cases, the market in which it operates.

Breakthrough results appear primarily in these four key dimensions: Profit, operating performance, company profile, and market position. Let's begin by considering the relationship between breakthrough and market position.

Figure 1.1
Breakthrough and Business Transformation

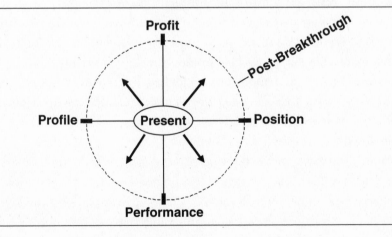

COMPETITIVE POSITION

Breakthrough can occur anywhere within an industry structure. The most common place to look for breakthrough in an industry lies at the entry point to the market. The cloud in the base of the chart below represents the chaos zone in which new entrants and venture companies test new business models for traction. Few succeed, but those who emerge from the cloud may reshape the market in the image of their breakthrough.

In virgin markets, the original innovator may swiftly progress from start-up to market champion in the absence of an established incumbent. Microsoft accomplished this feat in packaged software, Cisco in routers, Intel in microprocessors, and so on. Such firms can move through the phases from start-up to established market champion in a short time.

Although the chaos zone is fertile ground for breakthroughs, they can and do originate from anywhere in the industry. We have identified ten generic strategic positions that may be occupied within any industry. A single firm may occupy multiple positions over its life, but if it wants to move up, breakthrough is the bridge to higher positions. In the simplest scenario, a successful venture company seen at position A in Figure 1.2, transitions to the position of an insurgent growth company. Insurgent growth companies may receive substantial premiums in valuation relative to their limited market share, capturing a much larger share of the industry's financial market value. That premium will be short-lived unless the growth company can demonstrate ongoing gains in market share and the ability to scale itself into an emerging market leader. A growth company will either ride its breakthrough to the next stage in the success cycle or drop down to one of the states below it.

Figure 1.2 distinguishes between a mere market leader and a market champion. A market leader may ride a single innovation to a position of primary market share in its business. A market champion, however, not only holds the largest market share in its industry, but also holds a substantially larger share of the industry's total financial market value. Mar-

Figure 1.2
The Success Cycle

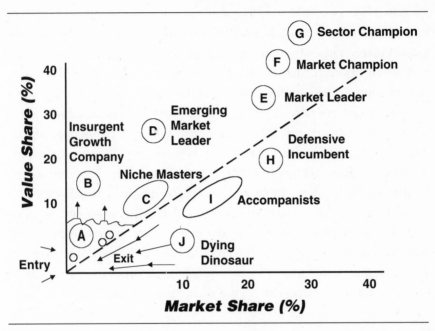

ket champions generally have demonstrated that they are able to retain their position of leadership and profit primacy over time in the face of new competitors and innovations. Also, many market champions look beyond their immediate market to expand into related markets and establish themselves as sector leaders and champions.

The lofty positions of market and sector champions mark the peak of the success cycle. These orbits, once achieved, are not sustainable without further rocket thrusts. Gravity is very much at work on market leaders and champions, who will inevitably slide into lower strategic positions without further breakthrough.

The declining phase of the success cycle begins when a firm retains market share leadership, but its value share falls below its market share level. Such defensive incumbents by definition face innovative insurgents positioned to seize leadership from the old lion. If the slide continues, the declining leader will join the pack of accompanists who exist in almost all industries. An accompanist competitor is one of the "me-too" players in the business who typically follow the lead of the primary players in the market place. They may make music, but someone else selects the song and sings lead vocals. Such firms are often the first to disappear via merger or bankruptcy during industry down cycles.

A secondary desirable destination in the corporate success cycle is the position of niche master. While more than one firm can occupy any of these ten generic positions at any time, it is common to see a significant number of niche masters in any industry. These firms have chosen to limit their playing field to an area of specialization in which they can compete successfully. Niche masters avoid head-to-head competition with the larger primary players in the marketplace, instead focusing on securing and defending a specialized success zone. Surprisingly, many of the most spectacular examples of breakthrough innovation and subsequent success cycles originate in the niche master zone.

BREAKOUT NICHE MASTERS

One of the very first breakthrough companies we spent time with turned out to be a classic example of a breakout niche player. Not long after the meeting in Emerson's library in Massachusetts, I attended another senior executive gathering at the Ojai Inn in California. The mood of this meeting could not have been more different from the setting in Massachusetts. Countrywide Credit was experiencing a breakout of unprecedented proportions. Its success cycle was just beginning. In the 1980s, it had been an established niche player in the home lending market, a wholesaler specializing in the resale of packaged loan portfolios to investment groups. As the decade of the 1980s wound to a close, it ranked 51st in U.S. loan volumes with some $1 billion in lending activity. Its market share was less than 1 percent. It might have stayed in its niche, but Countrywide had larger ambitions. In 1989 it launched a breakthrough strategy, creating a new division to market loans directly to consumers. With this new strategy, Countrywide also embraced an outrageous objective. It aimed to become the largest home loan provider in the United States.

Facing competitors more than ten times larger than itself, Countrywide could not and did not expect to compete on equal terms with the established leaders. It adopted a highly innovative business model designed to leap over the incumbents with superior speed, efficiency, service, and customer value. By the end of 1992, Countrywide would become number one in home loans, with more than $32 billion in loan volume—more than a twenty-fold increase in just four years. Now that's a breakthrough!

How did this company propel itself from the outer circle of the industry to market leadership in such a short time? It is a classic example of the power of breakthrough innovation. Countrywide provides its loan officers—called the "loan committee of one"—powerful online tools, including sophisticated decision support systems, access to third-party databases, automated application scoring, and the empowerment to finalize loans, often during the first conversation with the customer. Whereas the typical loan approval process at the time involved 14 or more discreet steps and parties, and industry approval times averaged between 40 and 50 days, a single Countrywide loan officer could approve loans in hours—frequently in minutes—at a fraction of its rivals' transaction costs. The industry cost for processing a loan application averaged approximately $2,350 in 1992. Countrywide's costs averaged about $750. Countrywide priced its loans very competitively for low-risk customers, and customers responded with enthusiasm to this new model. What knowledgeable customer would willingly submit to the traditional process with this new standard of service available? And indeed, the established industry leaders of the 1980s were all thrown from the hill as a new group of innovative lenders led by Countrywide seized market leadership. Of the top

Table 1.1
Top Mortgage Bankers
Ranked by Loan Origination Volume

1986	1992
1. Citicorp	1. Countrywide
2. CityFed	2. Prudential
3. Sears	3. Norwest
4. Goldome	4. Fleet/Norstar
5. GMAC	5. Chemical
6. Lomas & Nettleton	6. North American
7. Commonwealth	7. Sears
8. Fireman's Fund	8. NationsBank
9. BancBoston	9. BancBoston
10. Weyerhaeuser	10. Margaretten

Sources: *Mortgage Banking, American Banker, Inside Mortgage Finance.*

ten lenders in 1986, as seen in Table 1.1, only BancBoston and Sears remained in the top 10 just five years later. The insurgents had overcome the establishment almost overnight.

We have seen few examples in which insurgents captured the castle quite so swiftly and decisively as in the home mortgage lending industry. In this instance, a stable industry structure was torn apart in a few short years. Most incumbents have more time to prepare their defense. Here it seems many were displaced before they even knew what hit them. Several established players, notably Wells Fargo and Chase, rallied and returned successfully to the fray, but many others disappeared entirely as the market was redefined. As we shall see, today's home loan market leadership list reveals an interesting mix of agile incumbents who have successfully embraced the new order, and durable insurgents, notably Countrywide.

Many of the best examples of successful breakthrough originate in established niche players. We will examine Southwest Airlines, Progressive Insurance, and other powerful examples of breakthrough companies who burst out of their niches to capture leadership in the mainstream of their market, often redefining it in the process. The niche zone can be an excellent incubator for breakthroughs. Yet in every market, breakthroughs can appear from any of the ten generic positions, and insurgent competitors intent on capturing market leadership can emerge from any of these positions.

THE POWER OF BREAKTHROUGH

Breakthrough innovations fundamentally alter underlying customer service standards, cost positions, cycle times, and value propositions within a market, to the advantage of the breakthrough champion. Breakthroughs lead to differentiated, disruptive offerings that shatter the competitive equilibrium, creating space for the breakthrough company to gain or renew market share at the expense of its rivals.

Breakthroughs typically result from large-scale, long-term initiatives that use advanced technologies and radical process innovations to achieve leaps in operating performance, financial results, and market position. In the ideal state, breakthroughs result in multidimensional competitive advantages, leading to rising revenue growth, improved margins and profits, and increased market and value share.

Multidimensional Market Leadership

Breakthrough can result in simultaneous cost leadership, superior customer service, *and* product leadership. That pattern appears in dozens of the breakthrough companies we observed. Start with Countrywide Credit's experience: Its 1990 breakthrough in the home loan market reduced average transaction costs to $748, against an industry average of $2,357 at that time, enabling it to establish a position of extraordinary competitive advantage through cost leadership. At the same time, it was able to deliver dramatic improvements in customer service, specifically through reductions in loan approval cycle times of 90 percent or more, and by offering an integrated customer experience. It also offered additional product enhancements such as the opportunity to lock in interest rates at any point in the cycle. Countrywide claimed cost, service, and product leadership simultaneously, and the company translated its multidimensional competitive advantage into market leadership, moving from the bottom half of the top 100 home lenders to number one in the industry in a four-year period.

Southwest Airlines has been recognized as a customer service leader in the airline industry for years, complementing its documented cost leadership position. Both Progressive and United Services Automotive Assurances Company (USAA) exhibit a similar pattern of cost leadership and superior customer service levels in their parts of the insurance arena. The same pattern appears in manufacturing industries. Dell Computer has pushed industry leadership positions on unit cost, cycle times, and customer service levels in the personal computer business, for example.

These firms and more defy the statement that successful market leaders must focus on a single dimension of competitive advantage. Unidimensional competitors beware. Firms that possess some combination of cost, quality, cycle time, customer service, *and* product leadership in an industry pose a pretty good bet to secure dominant roles in their markets. Most firms who achieve breakthrough will find themselves in a position to convert the resulting multidimensional advantage into market leadership. Of course, competitive leadership is never static. Competitive dynamics ensure that leadership in any of these categories is a temporary phenomenon. Continuing innovation is central to sustained market leadership in any industry.

The Anti-Gravity Effect

Many breakthrough companies defy another mainstream management principle. When the right combination of factors come together, breakthrough companies are able to experience rising growth with increasing margins. At the simplest level, improvements in quality, service, and product features offer superior value to customers while cost and cycle time reductions drive improved margins. Progressive Insurance reported a return on equity of 22 percent during the 1990s against an industry average of 8.4 percent. During that decade its revenue growth rate more than doubled the industry average, and it increased its share of the auto insurance market by 500 percent.[2] Charles Schwab experienced even more dramatic growth in the 1990s. Its customer base grew from 1.3 million to 6.6 million, and assets under management increased from $25 billion to $725 billion, a compound annual growth rate of 45 percent for the decade. But during this dramatic period of growth, Charles Schwab's profit margins tripled from about 5 percent to nearly 15 percent (see Figure 1.3).

Figure 1.3
Schwab's Decade

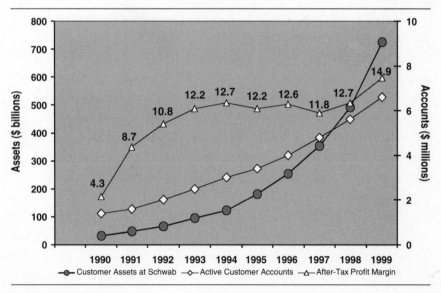

Source: Annual reports.

These results are characteristic of a breakthrough champion. Competitive advantages in cost, service, cycle time, and value proposition translate into revenue growth and rising market share, with increasing margins and profits. Rising operating and financial performance inevitably translates into a shift in market position.

Your firm can realize similar results. Market leadership comes to firms who are successful in achieving breakthroughs, whether the firm be an incumbent, insurgent, or other competitor. The first step is to focus your firm on a breakthrough strategy.

That reality may tend to favor new entrants. The new entrant carries no burden of financial and behavioral investments in legacy systems, processes, and organizations. Focused in pursuit of competitive advantage, new entrants seek out radical business models and processes. They may draw on technologies and techniques perfected in other industries, transferring them wholesale to a new field of application. New entrants are conduits for the groundswell of innovation that is driving business transformation in the 2000s and beyond.

Yet agile incumbents can seize these sources of innovation for themselves. In order to do so, today's champions must think about their business from the perspective of a new entrant. New entrants have no bond with the status quo. The new entrant cannot expect to succeed by adopting structures, practices, and performance standards similar to those already present in today's market. A successful new entrant must aim well beyond existing market standards. It must devise new strategies, offerings, and practices that will deliver substantially superior products and performance into an evolving market. To sustain their market leadership, today's incumbents must do the same.

If you are an incumbent, it is this mentality that must lead the transformation of your business. View your business as if you were an outsider. Remove yourself from both operating traditions and organizational context. The customer cares not two hoots about your internal structures and realities. Don't constrain your thoughts about market reentry plans by organizational limitations; organizational context is ultimately irrelevant to the shape of your future business. Your most significant competitors will suffer from no such self-imposed disadvantages. You must adopt this perspective or prepare for a diminished future.

The Starting Point

Successful breakthrough companies hold a set of attitudes and approaches in common. These core characteristics ultimately fall into two key categories—*strategic philosophy and principles,* and *leadership philosophy and practices.* We will begin by focusing first on the strategic elements that are common foundations for breakthrough. The path to breakthrough begins with these eight strategic principles, listed in Table 1.2.

Outrageous Objectives

Outrageous goals force us to consider alternative processes and technology platforms and thus foster breakthrough innovations. Here's a case in point from the auto insurance industry. Claims settlement has long been a source of customer dissatisfaction and defection in the industry. Many

Table 1.2
Breakthrough Strategy Principles

1. Pursue outrageous objectives.
2. Focus on the future.
3. Place primary emphasis on customer knowledge, care, and relationships, and secondary emphasis on cost reduction.
4. Emphasize process innovation over improvement of existing activities.
5. Use advanced technology to drive operating excellence.
6. Focus on a few critical core initiatives that span the entire enterprise.
7. Use human resources in new, creative ways with structured empowerment.
8. Identify and exploit new growth opportunities exposed by breakthroughs.

claims agents seem to view their job as protecting the insurer against fraudulent customers. Because the average insurance company earns all of its income from investments, they have little incentive to expedite payments. Customers often complain about the callous, uncaring attitude of claims personnel. Seeing an opportunity for differentiation, Progressive Insurance sought to provide the fastest and friendliest claims settlement services in the industry. Their initial efforts in the early 1990s included establishment of an 800-number that could be used to initiate settlement anywhere and anytime. Progressive invested over $30 million building PACMAN (Progressive Automated Claims Management System) to support expedited claims settlement. All personnel were sent through an empathy training program to help them focus first on solving customer problems. Implementation of this new approach reduced Progressive's claims cycle time to six days (against an industry average of 42 days), led to significant improvements in customer satisfaction, and reduced customer defection by two-thirds.

As these initiatives took hold, Progressive's management began to observe something very interesting about the settlement process: As cycle times shrank, so did the total cost of claims settlement. Faster settlement not only reduced costs in processing and administration, but it also led to lower litigation expenses, medical claims, fraud, and customer defection. Faster was also cheaper. This revelation led CEO Peter Lewis to establish an outrageous objective: Because faster was better for the customer and cheaper for the company, Progressive would settle claims instantly.

This outrageous objective—impossible to attain within the existing process—led to a series of innovations. Calls to Progressive's claims center now are relayed to a mobile van, which proceeds directly to the accident site. Upon arrival, the agent's first priority is to focus on the customer. An electronic image of the damage is transmitted to a central claims estimation unit over a wireless data network system, where the central unit uses an extraordinary knowledge base to estimate repair costs. Multilayered electronic engineering diagrams of more than 1,800 vehicles are used to determine repair requirements, options, and costs. The repair estimate is then transmitted back to the van, where a check is prepared, signed, and offered to the customer within an hour of the accident, in most cases.

Progressive's claims process reveals several important design principles. First, the process comes to the customer. Second, it is executed in real time, through a high-touch frontline supported by a high-tech, invisible infrastructure. Progressive designed the process to free field agents to focus on customer care, not claims estimation. Third, the claims process is designed to be customer-driven. Here's how it works: The agent offers the check to the customer and guarantees that if actual repair costs are greater than the amount shown, Progressive will take care of any additional charges. The agent then states, "However, my job is not to give you a check and wish you good luck in getting your car repaired. If you would like, I will arrange to have your car towed to a repair shop in our network. We will repair the damage, guarantee the quality of the work, and provide a rental car while your car is in the shop." The customer decides whether to accept the check or give the problem to Progressive.

Progressive's mission statement is the following:

> To be an enduring and profitable company by reducing the economic costs and human trauma of automobile accidents in cost effective ways that delight our customers.

The Immediate Response Service does just that. And like other breakthroughs, it exhibits dramatic improvements not only in speed and customer service, but also in cost reduction. When customers elect to have Progressive take care of the repair problem, the company is able to realize numerous cost savings. Its repair network, much like a managed healthcare network, delivers substantial discounts on repair procedures. The introduction of Progressive's software and communications links into repair shops dramatically reduces the cost of transactions between the company and the repair shop. Repair shop fraud is virtually eliminated. Superior customer service also drives down litigation costs and medical claims. Progressive's approach cuts the cost of repair in half while providing profoundly superior customer service. The company has leveraged this breakthrough to reposition itself at the front end of the food chain in the auto insurance business. Once exclusively a nonstandard (high-risk) insurance specialist, it is now breaking out of its niche and growing rapidly in the mainstream marketplace. Fueled by its combined cost and service advantages, Progressive now has a new outrageous objective—to be the largest auto insurer in the world.

Focus on the Future

We went to the ends of the earth to find a telephone company that was effectively transforming itself for the new era of online living. We only found one, in the most unlikely location—New Brunswick, Canada. New Brunswick is a poor province, with much higher than average unemployment rates and lower income than the rest of Canada. Its largest industries have been more closely connected to the hunting and gathering economy than the information age.

Hunting and fishing are still a large part of life in New Brunswick. In 2000, the province received more than 100,000 applications for moose hunting licenses. More than 97 percent of those applications were processed electronically over the NBTel network. If the moose-hunting world can make the transition to the electronic economy, any community can make that leap.

NBTel, a century-old incumbent provincial telephone company, now renamed Aliant Corporation, views its business as *electronic services integration*. The company focuses on creating what it calls electronic doors for delivering new services to its customers. These electronic doors are designed to be instant, interactive, and integrated. The doorways are also intended to be universal. In order to make enhanced services available to all of its customers, the company focused first in the early 1990s on providing electronic services via a low-cost display phone rather than by personal computers. By 2000, more than 60 percent of its customers were using the NBTel Powertouch phone. The screen phone gives customers access to a "call mall" of services from retailers, banks, and other vendors. The call mall delivers access to a number of electronic services including offerings from Sears, Royal Bank, Canada Trust, the Provincial Hunting and Fishing Department, Motor Vehicle registration, Cineplex Odeon, Orvis, and other retailers. Horoscopes and lottery services are also popular.

NBTel can deliver targeted text messages over the screen phone by interest category, postal code, and personal phone number. NBTel receives a few cents per message for these quick teaser ads. If the customer responds by pushing the "more" soft key on the telephone, NBTel receives an additional higher fee per response. If the customer goes further to hit the "call" soft key that connects the customer to the service provider, it receives an additional higher fee. Customer transactions with these service providers are tracked and recorded in a customer knowledge base to support targeted marketing activities. By 1997, revenue per display customer was almost double that of standard phone customers, at $49.85 for screen phone customers versus $28.65 per month for standard phone users.

Not only do display phones dramatically increase the revenue to the telephone company, but they also result in even more dramatic cost reduction benefits. NBTel Express was launched in 1993 as an extension of the ASAP service introduced in 1992 in provincial hospitals. ASAP was designed to allow patients in hospital rooms to initiate and terminate their phone service quickly and efficiently over the phone at any time, day or night. Now available on all display phones, NBTel Express allows customers to automatically activate or terminate service, request a service call, pay bills, add or delete features and functions, and purchase enhanced telecom services at any time.

While improving service levels, NBTel Express has also dramatically reduced its customer service costs. In 1992, NBTel's average transaction cost for each customer service request was $11.27 (Canadian). By 2000, NBTel had reduced its average transaction costs to less than $5 (Canadian), and self-service via NBTel Express accounted for more than half of all transactions. (The average customer service transaction cost for a U.S. telephone company today is about U.S. $20, and about a third of all customer service calls in the United States are repeat requests!) NBTel's average transaction cost in the year 2002 was $2.31 (Canadian), and 90 percent of all transactions were conducted via self-service over NBTel Express, furthering the company's mission to improve service while reducing cost. NBTel estimates that the average transaction cost for a self-service request over NBTel Express is 12 cents (Canadian).

While NBTel's initial efforts focused principally around its Powertouch display phone, it is also moving ahead aggressively with PC- and TV-based services. Whereas display phones featured a decidedly low-tech approach to transforming the telecom business, NBTel's new efforts focus on very advanced broadband offerings.

CEO Gerry Pond said the following:

> We can't survive as a narrowband telco, but we can't justify the investment of broadband on a stand-alone basis. This is not about introducing a new service; it's about transforming ourselves. The broadband network will allow us to reposition ourselves as an electronic services integration company. We can't do that on a narrowband network.

While other telcos are pulling away from their plans to build broadband networks, NBTel is pushing ahead aggressively. Other telcos have lost momentum amid indecision, technological uncertainty, and financial constraints. All continue to struggle with the immense investments and uncertainties associated with broadband. Amidst all this delay and procrastination, NBTel has charted a clear course and is making broadband services a reality in its marketplace. By 2002, its broadband network reached more than 60 percent of homes and 90 percent of businesses in the province.

Today NBTel's broadband network offers 10 megabit per second service to the household at the remarkable rate of $20 (Canadian) per month. On top of this basic bandwidth service, NBTel offers its Internet access gateway service and its VIBE interactive content service, each another $20 (Canadian) per month. The company currently holds about 70 percent of the Internet access market in the province—by far the highest market share for any telco in the Internet access business in North America. VIBE is its own content aggregator, with a base of proprietary and contracted third-party content, including games, sports, weather, and entertainment content.

NBTel's business model indicates that it expects each customer to purchase the broadband transport service, an Internet access service to connect to the World Wide Web, the VIBE content package, and additional interactive TV services. All of these services can be packaged by NBTel or built with third-party services as well. The company is now beginning to create what it calls its "videoactive network," which is comprised of all these elements. It constitutes the first true broadband electronic network in North America. NBTel considers the province of New Brunswick a "LivingLab" for electronic living. The provision of these various services as part of a broadband multimedia package is what NBTel calls electronic services integration.

Do you have to move to New Brunswick to enjoy the benefits of a true 21st-century network? No—NBTel is coming to you. In 1999, NBTel started a journey in that direction by merging with its three neighboring maritime province telcos to form Aliant Corporation. The new Aliant enterprise provides fertile ground for extending NBTel's success story to a larger population. Aliant recently crossed the border into Maine and

New Hampshire by forming Prexar, a provider of broadband Internet services in those states. Aliant is also developing vehicles to export its expertise and services to other carriers. Its Innovatia subsidiary develops services and applications that will be made available via other telecom carriers. Its mission is to "supply broadband IP [Internet protocol]-based applications to telecommunication companies, governments and other enterprises that are looking to provide new Internet-based service to their customers."[3] Innovatia and its sister emerging business units now account for more than 51 percent of Aliant's revenues.

Aliant is also active as an "electronic channel architect." It has established New Brunswick as an electronic transaction–processing center. More than 100 corporations have established transaction–processing centers in the province. NBTel assists these organizations in establishing state-of-the-art call centers. It provides sophisticated digital infrastructure backed up by redundant fiber optic loops and four disaster recovery centers, provides packaged computer-telephony integration services and customized call center applications, and delivers it all on a turnkey basis with full project management services. The number of call center minutes received in the province has risen from 181 million in 1996 to more than 1 billion in 2001, and traffic continues to grow rapidly. Call centers have created more than 10,000 jobs in the province and substantial, profitable additional revenues for NBTel. You may already be interacting with NBTel through one of these transaction centers such as HFS Hotel reservations (Ramada), Air Canada, and other airlines.

Aliant's effort to expand beyond traditional telecom service in the maritime provinces is bearing fruit. Revenues outside of Atlantic Canada exceeded 20 percent of total sales in 2001, up from almost nothing just a few years ago. Traditional local and long-distance voice services fell below 50 percent of total sales in 2002. At a time when other telcos are struggling to find a place in the 21st-century electronic economy, tiny New Brunswick Tel, now part of Aliant, is shaping and leading that new future. Says CEO Gerry Pond, "There is no reason that small towns and small people can't become big towns and big people."

By focusing on the future, Aliant is rapidly establishing itself as an emerging leader in the evolving telecom sector.

Use Advanced Technology to Drive Operating Excellence

Although it may be possible to achieve breakthroughs without the use of advanced technology, we know of few such examples. In particular, communication and information technologies tend to play a central role in breakthroughs. Whereas many organizations are slow to absorb and apply available technologies, breakthrough companies are not only early adopters; they are often heavily involved in the developmental stage of new technologies. Breakthrough companies frequently work closely with technology vendors to beta test and refine emerging technologies. These companies typically exhibit no more than average levels of investment in technologies and systems, but they concentrate more of that investment on leading-edge solutions in support of a focused strategy.

CR England, a Utah-based trucking company, personifies this approach. Like many breakthrough companies, CR England's renewal began with a crisis. Deregulation of the interstate trucking industry in the 1980s led to intense price competition and a wave of bankruptcies. A third of the largest trucking companies in the nation disappeared in just a few years. In the same time frame, the Department of Transportation cited England for safety violations. These crises forced the company to abandon traditional practices and philosophies and led it to become a technology leader in the trucking industry. Starting in the 1980s, England was among the first in the industry to deploy satellite communication systems in its trucks, enabling improved routing, scheduling, and customer service. In the 1990s, when Qualcomm introduced its second generation OmniTracks satellite system, CR England had the system installed in every truck in its entire fleet of 1,400 vehicles within two months. The new system not only provided more powerful location capabilities and two-way communications, but it also permitted monitoring of vehicle speed, fuel consumption, container temperature, and more.

CR England also led the industry in installing electronic data interchange (EDI) links that allow its customers to electronically schedule, monitor and pay for trucking services. Electronic invoicing has reduced the costs of billing from more than $5 to less than 15 cents per invoice. Electronic scheduling systems have helped the company meet its pickup and delivery schedules within a two-hour window more than 98 percent of the time. Tight coordination and communications allow England to play a growing role in the extended supply chains of its customers.

At CR England, superior service again coincides with lower cost. Its trucks now operate at a capacity utilization rate considerably higher than that of the rest of the industry. Moreover, due to mobile monitoring and maintenance innovations, it has increased fleet utilization by more than 1,000 miles per truck per month in the last five years. Freight miles per truck have risen sharply while costs per freight mile are falling with improved utilization. CR England, a private company, has realized sustained, superior profitability in an industry in which more than half the top 100 firms have disappeared in the past two decades.

The company's success is centered in what it calls MBI (management by information). The basic premise is that every activity will be monitored, measured, and managed to improve performance. CR England management believes that if it can be measured, it can be managed and improved. The company uses advanced information technologies in every aspect of its operations. Despite CR England's remarkable success, CEO Dan England said, "We need to move on to the next thing, we are getting into a rut." That mentality typifies breakthrough champions. Breakthrough companies are not interested in technology for its own sake—only in how it fits into a process context and in its ability to support the company's operating obsessions. CR England's obsession with every aspect of operating activity is typical of many breakthrough companies.

Preference for Process Innovation

Breakthrough companies focus on great leaps forward rather than on incremental improvements. This fundamental philosophy helped the oldest firm we observed achieve renewal in record time.

American Standard was the target of a hostile takeover by Black and Decker in the late 1980s. The company's management team, in partnership with the Louis Kelso organization, took the company private in a leveraged buyout financed by the creation of an employee stock ownership plan (ESOP) and extensive junk bond debt. The company took on billions in debt at an average coupon rate of more than ten percent. The loan terms precluded refinancing for at least five years. The company was laboring under this huge debt burden when North American housing construction plunged in the early 1990s. Faced with a financial crisis, CEO Emanuel "Mano" Kampouris concluded that funds for looming debt payments would have to be generated from internal sources.

Focusing on working capital and on inventory reduction in particular, the company introduced an innovative program called demand flow technology (DFT). Demand flow technology focuses on a make-to-order production model to eliminate finished goods inventory. Shifting from a traditional manufacturing approach that feeds a pool of finished goods inventory, American Standard moved to a system that only manufactures products in response to specific customer requests. In addition, the company worked to reduce work-in-process inventory by dramatically reducing cycle times for production activities. Kampouris called this program TNT, translated into Twice Net Turns. Its goal was to double inventory turns to free up $500 million in cash for debt-service payments to save the company from bankruptcy.

Kampouris canceled all financial incentives and replaced them with one: Every time working capital declined by $50 million, the company sent checks to 1,000 persons. By 2001, working capital as a percent of sales had fallen from almost ten percent to about two percent—a decline of more than two thirds. American Standard survived its financial crisis, refinanced its debt, and went public again in a 1995 offering. Kampouris then came forth with a new outrageous objective—to achieve negative working capital. These kinds of radical results can only be obtained through process innovation. Breakthroughs focus on creating tomorrow's processes, not on improving today's.

Emphasize Customer Care over Cost Reduction

Redefining the customer value proposition is central to all breakthroughs. Progressive Insurance redefined its relationship with customers by creating a superior customer relationship model. The result?—growing revenues, market share, and enhanced market value. USAA also began its life as an automobile insurance firm specializing in providing coverage for military officers and their families. A true market-centric firm, USAA's DNA is revealed in its response to market saturation. Having achieved a market share in excess of ninety percent for auto insurance in the military officer market, it chose to expand its range of offerings to its core customers rather than taking its core product to new markets. Because of its extraordinary customer service and satisfaction levels, USAA was able to expand its relationship with customers from its auto insurance base to a full line of insurance and financial services and more.

In order to manage this transition, USAA launched a breakthrough program in the 1990s with an outrageous objective. USAA aimed to complete every customer request and transaction in the first conversation with the customer. The operational goal was not cost reduction but rather customer service enhancement, for its own sake and to support expansion of customer relationships to new product lines. In order to achieve this objective, it created an integrated customer service approach that would support all of its product lines—auto, life, health, property insurance, and other service lines—and built new infrastructure to support it. The resulting enterprise information network gives service representatives easy online access to all the offerings, information, resources, and processes of the extended organization. Sophisticated call distribution systems route customer calls to appropriate representatives, and decision support systems enable rapid processing of customer requests and transactions. By 1995, more than 95 percent of all USAA customer requests and transactions—including claims—were completed in the first interaction with the customer.

Today USAA offers life, property, and health insurance and a full line of financial products and services to a stable customer base consisting of military officers and their extended families. A large and growing percentage of USAA's customers purchase more than one type of insurance coverage from the company, and a single service representative can now easily process multiple requests. USAA is a case study in how improving service can expand the customer relationship and ultimately—and profitably—grow the business.

Creative Use of Human Resources

Breakthroughs lead to fundamental redefinition of job descriptions and roles. Progressive claims agents went from working nine to five in a headquarters cubicle to staffing a mobile office 12 hours a day. Although these Progressive agents occasionally have uneventful days, more frequently they encounter medical emergencies, trauma, and other difficult situations in the field. Their jobs now resemble those of emergency medical technicians. Retraining people to fill such new roles is imperative to a successful breakthrough. Typically, however, the new jobs that breakthrough companies create are far more rewarding than are the old jobs they replace.

Loan officers at Countrywide Credit now have decision authority over loan approvals, where once they were once simply cogs in a larger machine. They have access to powerful supporting technology that enables them to process transactions quickly and efficiently while providing superior customer service. The results are satisfying on multiple fronts. Employees enjoy positive feedback from customers, higher compensation made possible by improved productivity, greater job autonomy and empowerment, and improved job security in a growing company. All contribute to greater employee satisfaction. Breakthrough companies capture their employees' imagination and commitment as they creatively redefine and enrich work activities.

Seeing and Seizing New Opportunities

Breakthroughs typically create unexpected new business growth opportunities. The more novel the technologies and processes developed in the original breakthrough, the greater the likelihood for business enhancement and extension opportunities. Yet these opportunities may go unnoticed and undeveloped without proper attention.

At Progressive Insurance, the original innovation in claims settlement not only led to a significant repositioning of Progressive in its market, but also may well yet lead to a dramatic redefinition of the auto insurance industry itself. Progressive is now launching a program to install electronic location devices in customer vehicles. These devices are designed to communicate with Progressive in the event of an accident, enabling the insurer to respond to customer needs even more rapidly. As these devices are installed in customers' vehicles, Progressive can exploit this new capability in a variety of ways. The ability to locate a customer's car can be used to recover stolen vehicles, for example, further reducing auto insurance costs and enhancing service to customers. The latest technology in this area combines global positioning system (GPS) satellite location with mobile communication capability, allowing not only vehicle location but two-way communication as well. This new capability could support a series of new services, including navigational aid, remote diagnostics, and security services.

Envision the following: a new core service that allows customers to contact Progressive in the event of an accident, breakdown, medical problem, carjacking, or other emergency. Progressive would then dispatch a mobile van to the customers' location to deal with the problem. This 21st-century roadside assistance service will change the center of gravity in the insurance industry from financial management to service delivery.

The insurance industry's traditional business proposition went something like the following: "When you buy our service we both hope you never need it, but if you do, contact us and we will meet you at some point in time and argue with you about financial settlement." The new proposition implicit in the emerging service model says, "When you buy our service, we both still hope you never need to use it, but if you do, contact us and we will come out immediately and solve your problem." The shift in focus from managing financial transactions to delivering services in real time promises to turn the insurance market upside down.

The insurance company's principal task now becomes managing a set of field service resources that are subject to unpredictable customer usage patterns. The customer is no longer just buying a financial protection service but also a claim on the company's service capacity. The center of gravity for the insurer moves to managing field service delivery and out of the hands of actuaries, accountants, and financial managers. For Progressive, this shift in focus to the front line has led to significant growth in the top line and the bottom line.

As the pioneer in this arena, Progressive is well positioned to lead in the development of this massive business opportunity. What led to the opportunity?—obsession with fast and friendly claims settlement, concern for customer care, experimentation with advanced technology and process innovation, and other core attributes of a breakthrough champion.

Management Magic

Breakthrough companies exhibit several hard-earned magical qualities. They routinely defy the gravity of mainstream management logic, especially traditional zero-sum thinking about business tradeoffs. It is widely held that improvements in customer service must necessarily entail increased costs and reduced efficiency. Executives are being told that they must choose between offering superior service and achieving cost leadership. This assumption often leads to primitive cost reduction programs driven by employee downsizing efforts that lead to diminished customer service and deteriorating customer and employee loyalty and retention. Our experience with breakthrough companies strongly refutes the existence of any mandatory tradeoff between efficiency and service levels.

Breakthrough initiatives routinely enhance customer service while delivering efficiency gains. Progressive Insurance provides customer service that is profoundly superior to its peers while cutting the cost of auto repair at the same time. USAA's customer satisfaction and loyalty levels are the envy of its industry, as are its costs. In-depth benchmarking might show that CR England operates with both the lowest cost-per-freight mile and the highest levels of customer service and satisfaction in its part of the trucking industry.

Breakthroughs smash traditional trade-off logic by offering radical gains in multiple dimensions of operating performance, improving productivity while enhancing customer service. They can also drive dramatic increases in velocity, improvements in accuracy and quality, and enable revolutionary levels of precision in the customization of products and services for individual customers.

Breakthrough companies tell us that a new definition of operating ex-

Figure 1.4
A Breakthrough View of Operating Excellence

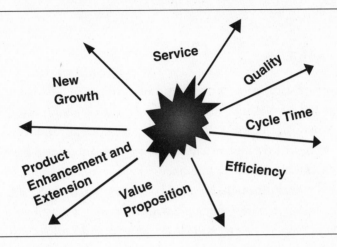

cellence is possible—one that denies traditional trade-offs and emphasizes leadership in multiple dimensions of operating performance. Yet
that is only one side of the diamond. Breakthroughs deliver not only
operating excellence but also significant business growth opportunities.

Breakthrough companies show that the pursuit of operating excellence in existing core businesses is intimately linked to growth in new areas. It is a powerful and positive paradox when sticking to one's knitting
combined with intense interest in the latest knitting technologies and
techniques leads to entirely new occupations. Breakthrough companies
typically exhibit an obsession with core operations and markets to the ex-
clusion of diversification activity. Yet—and here is the paradox—programs executed to enhance core businesses provide powerful platforms
for growth in new areas. Dig down deep enough into the details of your
operations, apply radical approaches, and perhaps you will break through
to the equivalent of China—a vast new market opportunity. The chal-

lenge then is to overcome the natural myopia that follows obsession with operating excellence to see and seize new opportunities. The result can be leadership in the core business *and* growth in new areas.

The Bottom Line

Breakthrough companies prove that traditional trade-offs between cost reduction and service and between focus on the core business and diversification may be illusory. Furthermore, traditional tensions between short-term return on investment and longer-term business growth may also be self-imposed. In many instances, the investments in infrastructure that underlie breakthroughs are paid back very quickly from immediate operating gains, providing free platforms for business development. The PACMAN system, built at a cost of some $30 million at Progressive, paid for itself in less than two years through streamlining of the traditional claims settlement process. It then served as a key platform for next-generation services.

At Blue Cross Blue Shield of Missouri, CIO Ed Tenholder and CEO Roy Heimburger pioneered a new service called Health Care Xchange in the 1990s. This service places PCs and insurance claims processing software in doctors' offices, clinics, and hospitals. The Xchange system allows healthcare providers to enter all of their claims into a single format and then converts these entries into the format of the appropriate insurance payer, and submits them electronically, streamlining and expediting the entire process. Investment in this new system was paid back within three years of introduction. The company's electronic presence in health care providers' facilities can now be exploited to introduce a host of enhanced services that may lead to the redefinition of the Blue's core business. This network can be used to provide patient insurance validation, precertification of procedures by insurance companies, prescription services, employee training, health records, patient referral, and scheduling services, and a wide array of other 21st-century health information services. Infrastructures developed in the initial phase of breakthrough programs hold powerful potential for long-term business growth. In short, management can have its cake and eat it too.

A fourth magical quality is evident in breakthrough companies. Breakthroughs belie the notion that stakeholders must engage in a zero-sum tug of war to extract benefits from organizations. Breakthrough companies seem to be able to drive increased benefits to all stakeholder groups at the same time. CR England has increased its truck driver population by almost twenty-fold in the last ten years, with one of the highest levels of compensation in the industry, while earning superior profitability and returns on capital, as well as dramatic gains in safety and customer satisfaction.

These enterprises are creating well-paying, rewarding employment opportunities; improving customer service and satisfaction; and delivering value to shareholders. No enterprise is fully future-proof, but these firms all have a firm hand on the evolving shape of their markets. All competitive positions are temporal, but the best breakthrough firms are serial killers. They offer ideal role models for aspiring market champions.

Breakthroughs transcend traditional business trade-offs. Breakthrough innovations enable firms to realize:

Cost *and* Customer Service Leadership
Operating Excellence *and* Growth
Core Business Vitality *and* New Business Development
Rising Revenue Growth *and* Higher Margins
Increased Benefits to all Stakeholders

Breakthrough innovation provides multidimensional competitive advantages and supports sustained market leadership.

NOTES

1. "Akers Cracks Down on IBM's Managers," from Associated Press, *Los Angeles Times,* May 30, 1991, p. D 13.

2. Source for Progressive's 1990 auto insurance market share: share of earned premiums, National Underwriter Property & Casualty/Risk & Benefits Edition, special report on auto and personal lines, April 15, 1991. Source for 1999 market share: share of net premium written, A.M. Best Co., *BestWire,* March 21, 2000.

3. Aliant Corporation 2000 Annual Report.

CHAPTER 2

THE ENTERPRISE PRINCIPLE

THE ENTERPRISE principle forms the backbone of every break-through company. It underlies and connects the *strategic mindset* and the *leadership philosophy* common to breakthrough companies. The enterprise principle differs sharply from management models that emphasize de-centralization, autonomy, and empowerment. Enterprise leadership phi-losophy emphasizes interdependence and adherence to a common core strategy. An *enterprise strategy* is a single, integrated master plan embraced and executed by all parts of the organization. Nothing is a better predic-tor of success in breakthrough initiatives than the commitment of the senior leadership team to driving a single strategy for the entire organi-zation. Breakthrough companies focus on large-scale initiatives that are implemented across the entire enterprise, transforming the firms' busi-ness and organization in the process. No factor so sharply distinguishes successful breakthrough companies as their one-minded commitment to a single, integrated game plan.

Such commitment is rare. It has been my experience that many so-called enterprise leadership teams are that in name only, and enterprise strategy forums are often mostly a combination of charade and negotiating sessions between independent business unit leaders. In pursuit of breakthrough, it is imperative that senior executives assemble to define and drive a common core enterprise strategy. Each must act for the best interest of the entire organization and not come to the table with his or her own narrow agenda. Unless this hurdle can be overcome, a breakthrough strategy is not a feasible option.

All successful breakthrough companies, large and small, exhibit the enterprise principle in action. But all firms who embrace the enterprise principle need not embrace breakthrough strategies. The enterprise approach can be critical to corporate success in other scenarios. In particular, companies operating in multiple related businesses who ignore the enterprise principle and pursue strategies of autonomy and decentralization place themselves at great risk.

DECENTRALIZATION DRAMA

In the mid 1990s, I spent several days working with Standard Oil of Indiana (Amoco). I remember asking the head of one of the larger groups about his management philosophy. His response to my question was, "My management philosophy is very simple. I set tough financial targets for my each of my SBUs, and I make sure they meet them."

I went on to ask him whether his group did anything to coordinate marketing, sales, and service activities to common customers. It turned out that they did not. Each SBU operated with autonomy in their marketing, sales, and service activities. I asked whether the group did anything to share upstream resources like billing, fulfillment, and other support functions. The answer was no. I asked whether the group did anything to share best practices across SBUs—no again. I asked the executive whether he had initiated any common programs or projects across the group. The answer in each case was "No—we set tough financial targets and make sure they meet them." This square-jawed individual was the single dumbest executive I've ever encountered.

But he was not alone. Amoco's senior leadership spent the decade of the 1990s "transforming" what was in essence a single business by decentralizing it into some 250 autonomous SBUs. Each of these businesses for the most part shared a common set of customers, suppliers, cost structure, technology platforms, and operating processes. Amoco took what was fundamentally one business and organized it to operate as more than 250 independent units. The results were inevitable, and when British Petroleum ultimately acquired the sinking Standard Oil Company, it chose to terminate the services of virtually all of the top 300 officers of the old corporation, executing a total transplant of the senior leadership team. Standard of Indiana stands as a benchmark—and not a positive one—for the absence of the enterprise principle both in strategy and in management mindset. Fortunately, we also have some positive benchmarks. Although it is rare, the enterprise principle can be seen in action at a number of leading companies. Perhaps the most visible benchmark is General Electric (GE).

THE GE MODEL

Jack Welch and GE stood alone at the top of the mountain in 2000. GE was the most profitable and valuable corporation in the world. It was a market leader—by mandate, number one or two in each of its businesses. Jack Welch was the most admired and imitated establishment CEO on the planet. GE's signature strategies—its portfolio optimization, performance culture, and Workout and Six Sigma programs—were being widely adopted in Fortune 500 circles by CEOs and companies eager to grasp some of the glory that was GE. At the core of GE's success, in my opinion, is a fundamental commitment to the enterprise principle. Ask Jack

Welch or any of the company's leaders whether GE is a holding company and you will get a sense of that commitment. Unlike Amoco, GE is in hundreds of unrelated businesses. It would seem to be an ideal candidate for decentralization and autonomy. Yet within GE, common core strategy principles and programs are embraced across the entire organization. Moreover, common leadership philosophies and practices were central to GE's success. GE's management and leadership model was designed and implemented with almost religious fervor inside the company, and it has won many converts in other corporations. The enterprise principle pervades GE's strategic initiatives and its leadership and management framework. It was not always the case.

When I was a young assistant professor at Dartmouth's Tuck school, GE was my first corporate client. My initial experiences at the old Crotonville training center were not positive. I particularly objected to the presence of alcoholic beverages in the classroom. In the 1980 time frame, the Crotonville learning experience could best be compared to a college frat house. I made a very visible departure from the Crotonville faculty. Perhaps that is why I was asked to return soon thereafter when executive development at GE was being revamped. GE had appointed a new CEO—someone completely out of the mold of its traditional leaders. Jack Welch was a heroic choice to replace Reg Jones, the previous CEO of GE. From day one, he made an extraordinary commitment to leadership development within the company. During my time as a faculty member at Crotonville in the 1980s, I do not recollect a single core executive development program at which Welch did not appear in person. Jack came to preach the "GE Way."

The GE Way was not so much about core strategy principles and programs as it was about management practice. The very first premise of the GE Way is that the company is an integrated enterprise and not a holding company. The enterprise was held together by common strategic programs such as Workout, Six Sigma, and change acceleration program initiatives, but the key binding elements in the GE enterprise model were centered around leadership philosophy and practice. Leaders were viewed as a resource of the enterprise and not of the local business unit. Emerging leaders—those on the A list—were perhaps more focused on their development path than on their current assignments. Welch spent an extraordinary amount of time with GE's human resources (HR) leadership team, and he was a personal mentor to hundreds of emerging leaders at any one time.

The GE Way was not negotiable. The performance management system developed at GE placed as much or more emphasis on conformance to the GE management philosophy and practice as it did on objective operating performance. The GE mantra, Right Results, Right Way, has become a mainstream management model. High performers who did not conform to the GE Way did not last long in this organization. I remember a conversation with Jack Welch in 1982 regarding an extremely bright young executive in the GE major appliance group. Jack had personally hired this individual from Booz Allen Consulting Company to come in and head up strategic planning for the Appliances business. When I raised this executive's name, Welch's immediate comment was "He is not a GE guy—he is too entrepreneurial." I believe that Welch could literally smell the personal qualities he wanted at GE, and he could tell almost instantly whether a person was GE material. I found it notable at the time that Welch and GE were not enamored of entrepreneurial executives. He was looking for an enterprise mindset. Those who did not meet this criteria were asked to leave the company. Although GE was very focused on operating performance, I believe that it may have been even more focused on conformance with management philosophies and practices.

In complete contrast to Amoco, GE took what were fundamentally 250 independent, unrelated businesses and made them into a single enterprise. GE defines one end of the enterprise spectrum. It exhibits common strategic principles and programs across the entire organization, and it embraces a common leadership framework and management model, yet GE is not a breakthrough company. It never embraced a core strategy in pursuit of an outrageous objective. GE's core strategy focused on maintaining market leadership positions through continuous improvement initiatives. Although it did launch enterprise initiatives by implementing Workout, Six Sigma, and other programs throughout the organization, it never adopted an enterprise breakthrough strategy in the full sense of the phrase, nor (with a few exceptions) did any of its business groups embrace breakthrough strategies. Its great success can be contributed primarily to its firm focus on an enterprise management model. It is my belief that if the GE leadership and management model could be harnessed in pursuit of a breakthrough strategy, almost anything would be possible.

Breakthrough companies exhibit a management mindset focused on an enterprise approach, á la GE, and a strategy focus on innovation and outrageous objectives. One might expect that companies with entrepreneurial cultures, who tend by nature to focus more on innovation, would be the source of most breakthroughs. Such firms can be effective at discrete or point product innovations, but they typically cannot achieve more fundamental transformation. As shown in Figure 2.1, real breakthroughs are best achieved when innovation occurs in an enterprise-focused organization. Let's look at why.

THE HEWLETT-PACKARD WAY

If GE symbolizes the enterprise mindset, perhaps one of the very best symbols of corporate entrepreneurship would be Hewlett-Packard. Hewlett-Packard built its success on a philosophy that emphasized autonomous business units created out of the entrepreneurial efforts of highly decentralized development teams. The prime career path at HP began with product development. HP's junior executives aspired to lead a development effort that would result in the creation of a new business unit, and the company has successfully focused and harnessed the entrepreneurial energies of its talented executive corps to do just that. The HP Way cre-

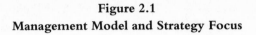

Figure 2.1
Management Model and Strategy Focus

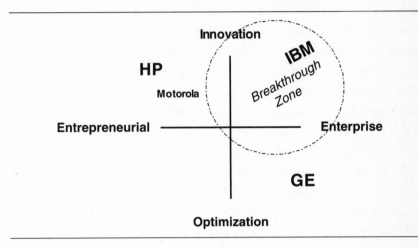

ated one of the world's greatest companies, but in the early 1990s this approach created serious difficulties in its computer business.

Hewlett-Packard's fifty-plus divisions operated as highly decentralized, autonomous units that largely defined their own directions: Thirty-six separate divisions had decided to enter the computer market, and each had designed and developed distinct product offerings. HP's highly entrepreneurial culture spawned a dysfunctional "family" of computing systems that used more than thirty distinct central processing units (CPUs) and more than thirty operating systems. It interacted with customers via a variety of divisional sales and service organizations. Corporate customers were surprised and disappointed to find that buying two computer systems bearing the Hewlett-Packard logo reduced enterprise connectivity and information sharing. In short, HP's excessively diverse technology base and product offerings placed it at a distinct disadvantage in the enterprise computing market as customers vocally demanded integrated computing solutions.

HP's response was to design a new-generation Reduced Instruction Set (RISC) computing family intended to replace all existing computing platforms with a series of products incorporating a single architecture and operating system. Its attempts to implement this new platform, however, were thwarted by the need to coordinate thirty-six historically autonomous product divisions active in the computing market, each with different market positions, technology platforms, and customer applications. Further examination revealed that HP owned and operated more than 100 circuit board assembly plants to feed its computing product lines, while the entire company's needs could have been met with only six plants. Each division had built its own capacity in manufacturing and many other areas without considering how to optimize the activities of HP as an enterprise.

HP experienced great difficulty attempting to migrate from its diverse technology, product, and organizational base to an integrated next-generation system. After several years of delays in implementing the RISC architecture, HP broke with its own made-here tradition and acquired Apollo Computer in an attempt to jump-start the changeover. Even that strong and uncharacteristic move could not overcome the underlying problem. HP was simply unable to sustain a leadership position in the enterprise computer systems business because of its culture of autonomy.

Salvation ultimately emerged from an entirely different quarter. HP's computer peripherals organization (CPO), which had been merely a fledgling business in 1990, introduced a series of printing products based on Canon's printer engine that vaulted HP into a leadership position in several segments of that market. HP's new-product introduction skills were then brought to bear, spawning a large number of successful new printer offerings, and HP quickly established itself as market champion in the desktop printer business. Over time, CPO gradually pulled together the various printer technologies, facilities, and products within

HP to create an integrated family of platforms and offerings. That itself was no small feat in HP.

Spinning discrete product technologies is the natural focus of highly entrepreneurial, autonomous enterprises like HP. The firm's entrepreneurial style facilitated its success in printers but kept it from becoming an effective systems vendor. Systems architectures require integrated enterprise efforts, a difficult act for decentralized firms to master. Hewlett-Packard ultimately turned its enterprise computing lemon into lemonade by building a consulting business that focused on—you guessed it—integrating diverse systems into enterprise solutions. Now a profitable multibillion dollar business, it has become one of HP's major growth vectors. Most examples of excessive autonomy don't work out so well.

Under Carly Fiorina, HP has focused its efforts on four core enterprise initiatives. One of its four core initiatives is called Value Chain Engineering, an effort designed to capture and integrate the diverse elements of any business that might be present within its independent divisions. Pulling together all these diverse, independent parts and organizing them into a single business begins with an enterprise perspective. Fiorina is also initiating a series of dialogues with senior executives about the HP Way. Much of the focus is on the theme of constructive collaboration between businesses. HP has also redefined its performance management system, ranking its executives on a five-tier grading system. On the scale of one to five, excellent operating performance will only get you a three. Highest-rated executives must exhibit constructive collaboration and conformance with the new HP Enterprise Way.

Conformance is not a polite word. I use it intentionally when I might be satisfied with using the term *alignment*. Why? Because there can be a hard edge to the enterprise principle. That hard edge can be seen in most breakthrough companies, especially in the second stage of a success cycle. I saw it clearly in action at a Countrywide Credit management forum in the early 1990s. During the session, Countrywide executives raised a series of new business development opportunities for the company. Given the growth of its retail mortgage business, it was envisioned that Countrywide could easily offer additional retail services such as insurance brokerage, escrow services, appraisal services, mortgage documentation products, and so on. All were good ideas, and all were built on the principle of exploring the adjacent opportunities exposed by any breakthrough. Many would ultimately become fast-growing lines of business for Countrywide.

Yet CEO Angelo Mozilo made it clear to everyone in the room that any further distractions would not be tolerated, and that anyone who was having difficulty staying focused on Countrywide's core strategy might find this an appropriate time to leave the company. I believe that it was this single-minded focus on their core strategy that enabled Countrywide to achieve leadership in home loans and to remain a leader as much larger competitors reentered the fray.

I've come to believe that there is a time in any corporate success cycle for Athenian-style democracy, in which creativity, innovation, free-wheeling discussion, and intense debate are desirable. There is also a phase in the corporate success cycle in which Spartan-style discipline and stoicism are necessary until the cycle starts again. That discipline is manifested in commitment to and conformance with core strategic initiatives and management practices. At GE, implementation of the Six Sigma enterprise initiative was announced formally in a memo to all business unit heads. All business unit leaders were to attend a two-week Six Sigma training class and launch the program in their units within six months. Failure to do so would result in a loss of their bonus and a year's worth of options, for starters. The larger consequence of management nonconformance was, of course, departure from GE. These initiatives were non-negotiable and not subject to debate.

The topic of tolerance for debate and distraction is one that arose time and again in my conversations with breakthrough leaders. In my debriefing sessions, I asked each CEO to reflect on what he or she would have done differently. The most common response, in summary, was "I would be less tolerant of distraction, debate, dissent, delay . . ." Underlying this fundamental issue is the enterprise principle. Corporate leaders must decide whether they are going to move forward as a single, integrated team or whether a philosophy of entrepreneurship, independence, autonomy, and decentralization defines the core of their company. Many firms seem unable to resolve this fundamental question of corporate identity. I have seen dozens of major corporations strategically disable themselves by failing to address the tension between enterprise strategies and the entrepreneurial instincts of business unit heads and other executives.

I was invited recently to meet the CEO of a major chemical company that was having difficulty implementing a shared sales and service platform for its fifty-plus independent business units. More than $300 million had already been invested in ERP and other platforms for this initiative, which promised to deliver much lower costs, higher levels of customer service, faster response times, integrated customer information, and more. The initiative defined the spear tip of a larger breakthrough strategy, yet the firm's independent business units were resisting adoption of the new system, stalling progress toward its new business model. After discussing what might be necessary to ensure timely transition to the new platform, including steps to require business units' adoption of the system, this CEO's response was "I don't think I can do that." This company's culture was committed to a highly decentralized management model, and conformance with a core enterprise strategy required a cultural transformation.

In pursuing an enterprise strategy, every effort must be made to communicate core strategies and principles and to align executives and employees with enterprise initiatives and practices. When alignment efforts fail, conformance may be demanded, and failure to conform must have consequences. Another CEO put it this way: He had just removed his best friend in the company, the general manager of the fastest-growing and most profitable division in the corporation, a great entrepreneur who

was unwilling to engage and collaborate with the enterprise strategy.
That CEO explained the move to his senior team quite simply: "No one
is bigger than the enterprise."

ENTERPRISE FIRST, BREAKTHROUGH SECOND

The choice between an entrepreneurial, decentralized management philosophy and an integrated enterprise approach was the fundamental issue
facing Lou Gerstner when he took over the reigns at IBM in 1993. Following IBM's meltdown in the fourth quarter of 1992, for the first time
in company history, IBM's board selected someone from outside to head
the company. When Louis Gerstner arrived from RJR Nabisco to take
the job of CEO at Big Blue, there was still much talk of the possibility of
breaking up the company to atomize the corporate bureaucracy and release the value of profitable or potentially profitable segments.

Some were calling upon Gerstner to decentralize IBM's operations in
imitation of the route the company took in setting up the IBM PC Company. Many IBMers in other segments were jealous of the PC Company's
relative autonomy. Gerstner, however, took another tack entirely. In
what he later described as his first "bet the company" decision, he decided to keep the company together.[1] Approaching IBM from the customer's standpoint, he determined that the answer was to reintegrate and
"to do a better job of packaging technology into workable, long-term
solutions for the customer." He focused on integrating IBM's business
units rather than dismembering them.

Gerstner created a Strategic Leadership Council, where the company's
senior leaders met regularly to develop and execute a common, core
strategy for the company. At the time, it was very difficult to focus on
long-term strategies. Short-term operating and financial pressures were
severe. IBM would shed tens of thousands of good and true employees
during a few short years; it was a very uncomfortable time. Some of these

realities were reflected in Gerstner's well-known comment early in his tenure: "The last thing we need around here is a vision." Yet what emerged was a visionary breakthrough strategy. Soon Gerstner would be talking about "our moon shot."

From Old Blue to New Blue

Gerstner's moon-shot strategy focused on bringing IBM's three core strengths together in a new business model centered on solutions and services. Those strengths—its customer base, technology portfolio, and people resources—were unparalleled in the industry. IBM used another unparalleled resource, its formidable training system, to retool its employees by the thousands to embrace and execute the new strategy. IBM's mainframe mindset systematically shifted to a solutions- and service-centered approach. Gerstner vowed the following in 1995:

> We're going to be the company that has the capacity to deliver total solutions and a multiproduct, multisector approach to the market . . . our diversity and our capacity to integrate will be a very powerful tool for us.[2]

The emerging services business was melded directly into the core of IBM's traditional business and organization. The services group was not allowed to operate as an independent entity. IBM's existing sales force drove the new offerings into the customer base. Existing units were driven to collaborate around customer-focused solutions. The new strategy was implemented at the core of IBM's traditional business. For example, the financial services sector sat at the heart of IBM's traditional business, representing about half of the company's profits. This sector and the sales and service organization serving it defined the very core of Big Blue. In 1995, Bob Howe, an outsider who had been brought in to head IBM's new consulting group, was appointed head of the financial services sector. His agenda was to drive the sale of solutions and services to IBM's core customers. Intimate access to IBM's sales channels and customer base powered the company's dramatic growth in services. By 1998, services accounted for over 50 percent of the company's total profits.

Innovation and Integration

Gerstner wasn't finished. In 1995, IBM created the Internet division to catalyze further change in the company. Gerstner described it in a comment that might have been used to describe IBM itself:

> The Internet is ultimately about innovation and integration. Innovation is what your objective is—in cost structures, selling, marketing, sales, supply chain. But you don't get the innovation unless you integrate Web technology into the processes by which you run your business . . . When you bring your company to the Web, you expose all the inefficiency that comes from decentralized organizations. Now, when a customer comes to you on the Web, they're expecting to move across these departments. They're expecting to see a common look and feel.[3]

Innovation around the Internet—IBM recorded the largest e-commerce revenues of any organization in the 1990s—further reinforced its integrated enterprise model. By committing the company to a newly integrated way of operating; by serving a more broadly defined customer base that included small- and mid-sized businesses; and by bending the organization to provide comprehensive services, networking, and e-commerce solutions, Gerstner enabled Old Blue to become Breakthrough Blue. With revenues of $108 billion and a market cap of $200 billion in 2000, IBM was once again Big Blue.

Lou Gerstner provided extraordinary leadership for IBM. He fundamentally changed the company's strategic direction, business model, culture, and management mindset. It may take an outsider to effect such dramatic change in an established organization, yet Gerstner was not a true outsider. He had close ties to IBM. Just two years before his appointment, as CEO of RJR, he had led a sustained collaborative effort with IBM to maximize the use of information technology at RJR. Gerstner was familiar with what IBM had to offer, especially from the customer's side. Furthermore, the IBM organization did not view him as if he were an outsider. His brother, Dick, had long been considered a candidate to head Big Blue before he was forced off the fast track because of Lyme disease. Lou was seen in a favorable light within the core of the company; moreover, Gerstner's style was also a great fit with the IBM culture. He was customer-centered, practical, and principled. He was the stable hand on the tiller during turbulent times; however, Gerstner's key contributions were two momentous decisions: his commitment to an enterprise approach and his choice of a breakthrough strategy. Those choices and his personal leadership are what transformed IBM.

IBM had to experience a severe business crisis to become a breakthrough enterprise. The severity of that crisis forced IBM to make tough decisions about becoming an enterprise and embracing a big-bet breakthrough strategy at the core of its being. Most companies, try as they might, can't make it over these fundamental hurdles. Here's how another great company in crisis approached this challenge.

MOTOROLA

Motorola has been recognized as one of the world's great corporations by many observers, yet in the late 1990s the company experienced a downturn of dramatic proportions, even though it was positioned at the heart of one of the great growth industries in the global economy. In losing its market leadership position in cellular phones to Nokia and Ericsson, Motorola's market share fell from nearly 50 percent to around 10 percent in just a few years. How did this happen? Give Nokia and Ericsson credit, but this story is more about leadership lost than gained. No major corporation has been more committed to decentralized empowerment than has Motorola, and therein lay the problem.

Motorola had built a culture based on rampant—if not rabid—entrepreneurial activity. Famed for its "warring tribes," Motorola's culture promoted internal competition even within its many tribes and clans. That competition was nowhere more apparent than in product development. Would-be product champions engaged in intense competition for budgets, engineering manpower, and other resources to feed product development efforts. The problem was that hundreds if not thousands of individuals pulled Motorola's product development activity in a multitude of competing and often conflicting directions. Compounding the chaos, Motorola had no common product development or quality assurance processes and—most important—had disjointed or nonexistent group and corporate product portfolios and roadmaps.

In contrast to IBM's famed "shoot-out" exercise between competing technologies, products, or solutions, Motorola had no structured process for managing internal competition. Without a formal process, wannabes and losers lingered around while winners failed to reach critical mass. Many redundant initiatives consumed vital resources while critical programs languished, and obvious if unexciting opportunities were ignored altogether. Everyone was too busy doing his or her own thing to notice that this company was in trouble. Motorola was dissolving into chaos.

In 1998, sensing that these many centrifugal forces were pulling the company apart, scion Chris Galvin, along with key executives Bob Growney and Merle Gilmore, took the drastic step of pulling together all its cell phone, wireless, satellite, and cable modem business units into a new communications enterprise (CE) group. CE was charged to create a common look and feel for all Motorola's wireless products, a common brand identity, a single strategy for the entire CE, coherent product planning and development roadmaps, common technology platforms, and integrated network equipment offerings. The stakes were huge. Motorola aimed to reestablish itself as the leader in wireless communications, and it had a lot of ground to make up. Motorola's new enterprise strategy for its wireless businesses created a set of critical common priorities, including the following:

- Regaining market leadership in cellular access devices
- Achieving industry leadership in profitability and growing revenues faster than the industry
- Implementing new core processes for CE, including common strategic planning; supply chain, marketing, product line planning; product development; and quality assurance processes
- Developing common product platform strategies
- Maintaining clarity and consistency of vision
- Achieving strategy alignment and deployment
- Supporting executive adherence to "rules of engagement"
- Ensuring collaboration between business units

These new priorities described a fundamental shift in Motorola's management world. Its new approach emphasized enterprise strategies, platforms, processes, and management practices. Note the emphasis on collaboration, common platforms and processes, alignment, and adherence to the new "rules of engagement." These new rules place the customer and the enterprise ahead of the business unit and individual interests. Motorola redefined the contract between the company and its executives, and it reset the limits of autonomy and empowerment within the context of a common enterprise strategy. The basic principle is a simple one—the enterprise comes first.

New Initiatives

One important new initiative established a program management office within CE, staffed with more than 400 project management professionals, to ensure disciplined execution of key initiatives. Motorola's transformation included expansionary thrusts in several new directions as well. Long a product-centric company, its unidimensional product innovation focus had led it to neglect the market and customers in favor of a focus on products and technologies. To reverse this imbalance, the company formed a new group called the Services and Solutions Organization (SSO) within CE specifically to focus on repairing and building relationships with key customers. But Motorola was not only intent on renewing its existing wireless business. It also established a new business unit to capture market leadership for Motorola in the emerging wireless Web world. This unit, the Personal Networks Group, was created from whole cloth under Janiece Webb, formerly head of Motorola's Network Services Group.

Webb is not your average high-tech executive. The highest-ranking woman in Motorola, she is a miner's daughter from rural Arizona who started out on the production line in a Motorola semiconductor plant—on the night shift, no less. An engaging person of extraordinary IQ and EQ (emotional intelligence), she worked her way up the ranks. Given responsibility for a set of paging service companies, including a number of bankrupt operators who had defaulted on their equipment payments to Motorola, she built and later helped to sell the multibillion-dollar network services group. Felled for two years in the mid-90s by serious illness, her return to the fray in itself was a great personal achievement.

Webb and her team set out to create a master plan for market leadership in the wireless Web arena. The plan identified all the key elements of the wireless Web market, including wireless servers, content distribution networks, location systems, synchronization technologies, unified messaging, electronic agents, and end-user applications. Webb and her team then set out to build or buy all the major elements to support an aggressive market leadership strategy. Moving on multiple fronts, Motorola's actions included the following:

- Buying the research and product development section of Lucent Technologies' wireless handset group
- Acquiring majority stakes in a series of U.S. and European wireless ventures
- Purchasing from Hyundai a 1.1 million-square-foot semiconductor factory in Scotland, for refitting to produce semiconductors with "smart" DigitalDNA wireless technology—a $2 billion investment
- Building and deploying the Aspira edge server network for pushing content into wireless devices
- Crafting a four-year, $1 billion pact with Cisco Systems to migrate wireless phone traffic from voice switches to routers capable of handling voice and Internet data
- Developing the MIX wireless web server platform for deployment in their own and third-party carrier networks

The firm spared no resources in supporting this aggressive program. By 2001, Motorola began to show critical mass in this space, realizing significant progress toward its goal of becoming market leader in one of the most promising growth markets of the 21st century. Will this become the start of a new success cycle for Motorola?

Implementing an enterprise strategy and management model in a highly entrepreneurial culture is a very difficult feat. Motorola's attempted transition from rampant decentralization to an architected enterprise approach was traumatic. Turnover among its talented executive ranks soared in the face of new disciplines. Tension between traditional entrepreneurial forces and the new enterprise focus remains high, but strong leadership, extensive training, a new strategy process, and a new performance management system all helped contribute to Motorola's ongoing transformation. Will it take? In 2001, Motorola spun out Janiece Webb's unit, the Personal Network Group, and the SSO group from the CE core. These two new units will benefit from greater freedom to focus on their development agendas, but will they retain a strong sense of enterprise alignment from their formative years in CE? Will the next-generation business build on and integrate with the traditional core business? Or will Motorola's warring tribes reappear? What is the right balance between entrepreneurship and enterprise? All these questions remain to be answered by Motorola, and the same issues are present in every company to some degree.

THE ENTERPRISE WAY

The enterprise principle applies not only to large, diverse firms. Some of the best practitioners of this approach are entrepreneurial, Silicon-Valley–style venture companies. The venture capital community generally insists on pure plays. You don't ask a venture capital firm for funding with a plan that says, "We're going to do A . . . , and B . . . , and C." They demand total focus on a single target and build portfolios of such one-trick companies. *Venture companies by nature pursue a focused core strategy in pursuit of a single outrageous objective.* The fact that everyone from the CEO down wears T-shirts and sandals should be viewed not as an iconoclastic statement but rather as a sign of conformance to a strong corporate culture and leadership framework. Venture firms often exhibit less diversity than do larger, established organizations.

Where does your organization stand on the enterprise spectrum? Where do you want to stand? The first question you might ask yourself is, "Are we an enterprise or not?" The real issue here is one of choice— a critical choice in defining your core corporate identity. Many factors must be considered in making that decision: business diversity, competitive conditions, customer requirements, and so on. But this aspect of corporate identity has more to do with business philosophy than with market requirements. Look carefully: you have already made a choice.

Begin by examining the dynamics of your senior leadership team. In successful breakthrough companies, senior leaders tend to spend a significant amount of their time together as a team. Typically, this team includes the top ten to twenty executives, who operate as a close-knit social system. They are more likely to meet weekly than quarterly. The resulting alignment of this group shows up in a number of important areas.

A strong enterprise leadership team improves the quality, richness, and cohesiveness of the company's core strategy. Strong enterprise leadership increases the ease and speed of decision making. Companies whose senior leaders function as an enterprise team are able to process decisions much more quickly than are organizations who exhibit higher levels of autonomy. Decisions are made more quickly and effectively when they are examined through a single enterprise lens and not by the narrow self-interest of individual units within the organization. More important is that having a clear, single enterprise strategy means that any incremental decision can be readily evaluated in terms of its fit with the company's direction. Rapid and effective decision making also translates into ease of execution because of the high degree of senior team alignment in support of a common strategy. In contrast, companies in which the enterprise principle has not been developed may exhibit the following:

- Almost exclusive focus on financial results
- Lengthy decision cycles and extensive analytical effort
- Primary emphasis on financial justification for new project decisions
- Many partially completed projects
- Severe competition for internal bottleneck resources
- A tendency to internalize key functional resources within individual business units
- Extraordinary pressure on key resource gatekeepers
- Frequent escalation of conflict to senior management
- Proliferation of different infrastructures, systems, and processes

- Difficulty in coordinating across multiple infrastructures and systems
- Local career paths for promising executives
- Senior management meetings dominated by internal resource allocation decisions
- An inability to scale local innovations
- High stress and poor management morale

If you are experiencing these conditions, your best investment will be in building an enterprise foundation in your organization. That means building both an enterprise strategy and an enterprise leadership framework.

Enterprise strategies can begin with common core principles such as GE's commitment to be number one or two in each market it serves. Enterprise initiatives, common programs implemented across the entire organization, mark another step in the enterprise hierarchy. Company-wide execution of core initiatives such as Six Sigma, quality improvement, or cycle time improvement programs constitute a meaningful commitment to the enterprise principle. The ultimate enterprise strategy is a single master plan with specific core initiatives implemented in an integrated fashion across the organization. When that single strategy commits the enterprise to the pursuit of an outrageous objective, breakthrough can happen.

The best place to start building an enterprise is in the senior leadership team. Investment in an enterprise leadership framework starts by focusing the company's senior team on becoming a council that functions to drive the organization toward its highest and best state. It is no small feat to shift the focus of a senior executive team from their narrow responsibilities to the best interest of the overall enterprise. One of the masters of this art is Jere Stead, who led Ingram Micro through an extraordinary period of growth in the late 1990s. I worked closely with Jere when he was the head of the Business Products Group at AT&T in the mid 1990s. He had assumed leadership responsibilities for a group that had been losing money for several years. The top execs in this unit seemed to be more focused on their rivals within the group than they were focused on the external competition. Unable to secure any alignment among the senior team and frustrated at the failure of team building exercises, Jere received a suggestion that he consider repopulating the senior team. Jere rejected that recommendation and focused instead on creating a new "contract" for his existing senior team.

At the next meeting of his top 40 executives, he announced the termination of the existing bonus plan and its replacement by a new set of incentives. The top 40 executives would share a single set of incentives and a common incentive pool. No bonus payments were to be made in the first year, but if incentive targets were achieved in the second year, each of the executives would receive a multiple of his or her base salary. However, each of the key targets had to be met in full for anyone to receive any bonus payments at all. This new incentive system sent a clear set of messages to the senior team. First, they had to be committed to the long-term success of the group. Second, they had to work together to achieve a set of enterprise targets that required close collaboration and coordination among the various parts of the business. Third, they had to function effectively as a team in order to succeed and to be rewarded. This new incentive system, combined with Stead's extraordinary one-on-one coaching capacity and his persistent focus on the new targets, led to an almost immediate and dramatic improvement in results. The group's tailspin rapidly reversed itself, and it went on to significant growth and profitability in ensuing years. Stead went on to achieve extraordinary results at Ingram Micro, growing it from revenues of $8.6 billion in 1995 to more than $30 billion in 2000, making it the market leader in high-tech distribution.

As you can see in this example and at IBM, GE, and others, so much of the success of an enterprise approach depends upon the CEO. We discuss more about enterprise leaders in a later chapter. From strong

CEO leadership and a cohesive senior leadership team, a series of other enterprise characteristics follow. A strong enterprise should exhibit the following:

- Common strategic principles; programs; and in the ultimate form, a single core strategy
- A common leadership framework, with a centralized approach to leadership development
- A common management philosophy and common policies and practices
- A common culture
- Integrated infrastructure and systems
- Integrated processes
- Common targets and obsessions

Remember, these characteristics alone do not make a firm into a breakthrough company. The next questions you may therefore ask yourself are, "Do we have a breakthrough strategy? Do we want one?"

NOTES

1. Ira Sager, "Gerstner on IBM and the Internet," *Business Week,* Dec. 13, 1999, p. EB40.

2. Ira Sager, "We Won't Stop . . . Until We Find Our Way Back," *Business Week,* May 1, 1995, p. 116.

3. Sager, "Gerstner on IBM."

CHAPTER 3

THE STRATEGIC SETTING

THE FOUNDATIONS of a sound strategy are self-knowledge and knowledge of the external environment. Self-knowledge not only covers your resources, current profile, and competencies, it also includes your core identity. A clear sense of corporate identity focuses and simplifies any strategic decision. Here's an example: GE does not participate in short-cycle, high-tech businesses. In the past decade or so, it has systematically sold its short-cycle businesses, including consumer electronics (TVs) and semiconductors. Such industries hold no attraction because they fundamentally do not fit with GE's strategic and managerial identity. It has a clear understanding of where its strategic and management model works best and where it is not effective. GE focuses its efforts on building and maintaining market leadership positions, typically in stable (if not mature) capital-intensive industries. It is capable of making big bets in zones that fit its identity, but it studiously avoids those requiring other competencies, strategies, and management models.

Similarly, many entrepreneurially inclined organizations may best avoid large-scale, integrated systems opportunities. Motorola, an adept product innovator when it comes to consumer communications hardware, has never been able to crack the code when it comes to network switches and infrastructure equipment. Understanding yourself is central in shaping a sound strategy. In that light, firms with a decentralized management model are poor candidates for breakthrough strategies.

The primary prerequisite for pursuing a breakthrough strategy is the capacity to focus on a single core strategy for three to five years or more. Continuity in senior leadership during that period is particularly important. Those are the key gating factors in choosing to pursue a breakthrough strategy. Resources are not really a limiting factor, although midsized firms with a relatively narrow business portfolio seem to be particularly fertile ground for radical strategies. They may possess a combination of resources, agility, and focus unmatched by smaller and larger firms, but breakthroughs occur in small and very large firms as well. Age does not seem to be a limiting factor. Three of the five firms who executed their transformation strategies most effectively and expeditiously were more than 50 years old (American Standard, Aliant, and IBM).

Breakthroughs can originate from anywhere in an industry. The fundamental question is who has the insight and gumption to shape and launch a breakthrough strategy in any market and the persistence to stay focused as a team to execute it. Transformation requires not only a brilliant, innovative strategy, but also faith, focus, fortitude, and more: These are the internal realities of breakthrough.

Even if you have what it takes, you should ask the following questions: Is a breakthrough strategy feasible? Is it desirable—and in some cases—is it necessary? Start by considering these generic options as presented in Figure 3.1:

- Maintaining your current position and profile and presumably current performance and profit results

Figure 3.1
Corporate Strategy Options

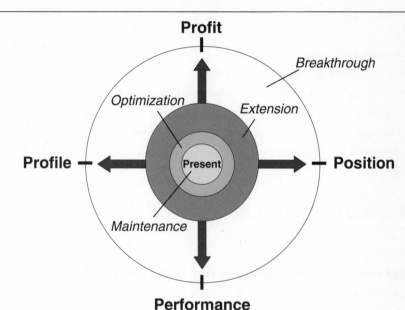

- Initiating efforts to optimize current performance, profile, and position and thereby improve profitability
- Pursuing incremental expansion or improvement in products, markets, channels or operating performance
- Pursuing a radical strategy in pursuit of outrageous objectives to dramatically improve performance, reshape the firm's profile, shift its market position, and achieve powerful gains in financial results

Few firms enjoy the luxury of being able to choose a maintenance strategy. Only near the peak of a success cycle or in very hypocompetitive markets and niches will such strategies prosper. In most settings, market trends will erode the effectiveness of even the most successful strategy foundations sooner rather than later. In the extreme, hypercompetitive markets require almost constant innovation. In such settings, radical strategies may be the only feasible option. Industries undergoing fundamental transformation will not support maintenance, optimization, or incremental strategies. Many breakthrough strategies are launched because they are the only feasible option facing an organization.

The decision to embrace a breakthrough strategy must rest on two fundamental conclusions: first, that the internal realities of your organization will support focused, sustained pursuit of a radical strategy; and second, that such a strategy is feasible in light of external realities.

COMPETITIVE CONSIDERATIONS

Before you set your sights on a breakthrough strategy, examine the external environment with great diligence. Radical strategies are not a wise choice for all firms. Breakthough can occur in any market, but aggressive aspirations are not always appropriate. Competitive factors are critical in both choosing and crafting a breakthrough strategy.

Competitive strategy formulation begins with a grasp of the generic—a fundamental understanding of the core competitive positions, roles, structures, and dynamics that appear in every industry. All strategies, radical or otherwise, must be formed from this perspective. Aspiring companies must first map their market to identify the competitive conditions present in the business. Start by examining the positions and movement of competitors relative to the success cycle chart presented earlier. Identify which positions are occupied and the status and trend line for the key players in the market. The most important place to start focuses on the role and status of the market leader.

The Lion's Share

A healthy market leader will capture a share of industry value that is even larger than its share of the market. A value share to market share ratio in excess of 1.0 indicates a vigorous, active leader with highly developed competitive strategy skills. Firms that can sustain such positions are true market champions. The list of lions includes many household names—Intel, Microsoft, and Wal-Mart for starters.

Wal-Mart is the world's largest retailer with 2003 revenues and market capitalization approaching $250 billion. The storied retailer far outpaces its competition in both market share and value share, capturing almost 50 percent of its peer groups' market share and almost 75 percent of the group's value as shown in Figure 3.2. Viewed from this perspective, other retailers like Target, Sears, and Costco are reduced to fighting for table scraps.

Market leaders in other industries aspire to and sometimes achieve such dominance. But winners include more than the few firms who lay claim to the lion's share of industry value. Take another look at the pack via the ratio of value share to market share—this time eliminating Wal-Mart's scale-distorting presence from the chart, and a second winner emerges at the other end of the market share spectrum.

Kohl's stores established a unique niche selling upscale department store brands of apparel, footwear, accessories, and home furnishings at moderate prices (and with a discount-store cost structure) in an attractive atmosphere. Kohl's carries such brands as Nike, Levi's Dockers, Champion, and Krups at a ratio of 80 percent brand names to 20 percent private-label goods compared to 50-50 at Sears and J.C. Penney.[1] Its 80,000-sq.-ft. stores tend to be smaller and easier to navigate than are those in department or discount stores. They are often located in stand-alone sites and feature wide aisles, prominently displayed fashion items, and pleasant ambience. Its 300 stores have a narrower selection of products than a full-line department store does, but the company makes a point of carrying

Figure 3.2
General Merchandise Retailers:
Market Share and Value Share

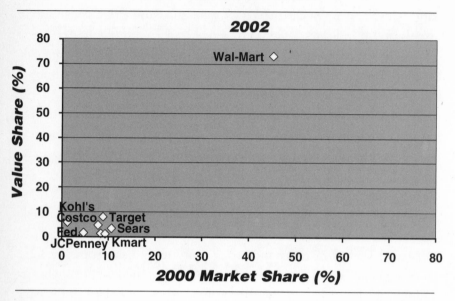

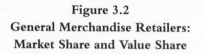

deep stock in sizes and colors of those products it does carry. Kohl's sells a higher-than-average ratio of merchandise at nondiscounted prices.

At first modeled after West Coast value department store Mervyns, Kohl's focused on selected segments: apparel and furnishings. Selling recognized brands at a discount, Kohl's developed a niche between mall-based department stores like Macy's and Sears and suburban big-box discount retailers like Target and Wal-Mart. Although sales approaching $5 billion are dwarfed by those of Wal-Mart, Sears, Target, Kmart, and others, Kohl's revenues, profits, and new store openings are all growing strongly. As shown in Figure 3.3, with a mere 1.25 percent share, Kohl's has captured roughly 6 percent of total market capitalization among competing retailers. Niche master Kohl's ratio of value share to market share, at more than 450 percent, dwarfs not only that of a retail success

Figure 3.3
General Merchandise Retailers:
Market Share and Value Share

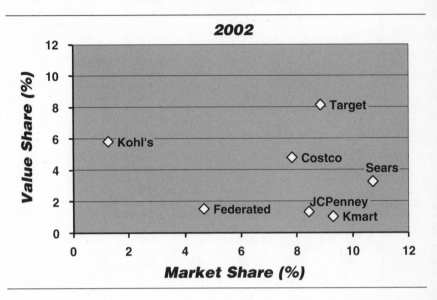

story like Target, but it is also three times that of the market champion, Wal-Mart. A well-managed niche player can garner substantial value share even in a traditional industry that otherwise seems to be, for all intents and purposes, locked up by the Arkansas retailing behemoth.

Value Distribution

The general merchandise retail industry provides a useful generic profile of industry value distribution. A dominant industry leader is awarded a premium valuation—the lion's share. Successful niche players or insurgents are also awarded a premium in value to market share, leaving all the firms in the middle of the pack at a discount. The profile in Figure 3.4 represents a common pattern seen in many industries. The pattern may

Figure 3.4
Market and Value Share

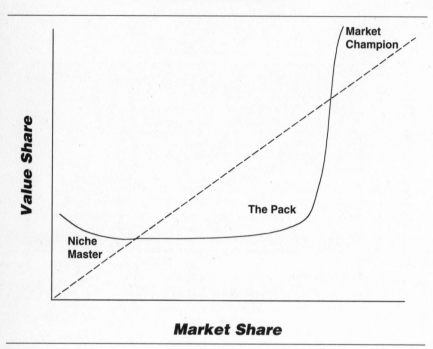

Market Share

even be stable if profitable niche firms limit themselves to defensible segments and if the market leader aggressively maintains its advantage over the rest of the industry.

Evaluate conditions in your target market, the position and trend lines for other participants, and your own position before selecting a strategy. A second framework can help in that regard.

Competitive Strategies, Concepts, and Tools

A related framework, developed by Professor Jagdish Sheth of Emory University, provides a useful perspective on underlying competitive ar-

Table 3.1
General Core Competitor Strategy Profile Elements

- A full line of product and service offerings in the market
- A well-known and valuable brand name
- Broad market coverage
- Broad channel coverage
- A full field sales and service footprint
- State-of-the-art technology assets
- Comprehensive R&D program
- Vertical integration in key areas of the business value chain
- Horizontal integration of the value chain

chetypes and dynamics. Sheth's framework distinguishes between "inner-circle" and "outer-circle" competitors in any given industry. Inner-circle firms compete on the basis of maximum scale and scope. They exhibit a generic strategic profile that includes a number of core elements.

The profile in Table 3.1 depicts the classic incumbent market leader. Necessarily, it involves substantial fixed costs. National—much less global—brand recognition entails hundreds of millions of dollars in advertising and related expenditures. A field sales and service organization cost even more, and annual R&D expenditures in any major technology sector run into the billions. An inner-circle strategy is a very expensive proposition. The high fixed costs associated with this generic strategy leads to a key conclusion.

Bruce Henderson, founder of the Boston Consulting Group, first formulated the *rule of three* in the 1970s—the principle that a stable market never supports more than three significant competitors. Sheth also holds that any mature industry will support no more than three profitable inner-circle strategies. This rule of three stands on the premise that a minimum of 10–20 percent market share is required to generate sufficient margins to support a market leader's strategy profile and fixed cost structure in the typical mature business. It holds that as industries mature and competitive dynamics play out, any industry will support no more than three players with sustained, profitable inner-circle strategies. Although the cost elements and timeline may vary, the rule of three appears to hold across a wide range of industries.[2]

In the early stage of industry evolution or globalization, five, 10, or more firms may vie for market leadership. The list of credible contenders generally shrinks to seven or fewer during the growth phase of the industry life cycle. As the industry begins to mature, the rule of three applies in force, and a related rule of thumb may prevail: Inner-circle competitors generally hold 60 to 80 percent of total market share, with the remainder claimed by outer-circle niche competitors.

It is possible to observe more than three inner-circle participants even in mature globalized industries, but few industries will support more than three firms with sustained profitability. Typically, one or more of the extra participants is part of a parent company willing to subsidize prolonged unprofitable operations. The television broadcasting business in the United States held three profitable inner-circle players for many years. Over the past decade, as Fox TV pushed into the inner circle, only one of the four core firms has been consistently profitable—NBC. Disney has supported ABC, Westinghouse and then Viacom subsidized CBS, and Newscorp fed Fox. It is not uncommon for marginal inner-circle participants to be subsidized by a patient parent company, be it Japanese, Korean, European, or American, enabling the presence of more than three major inner-circle competitors; that does not defy the rule. The economics of most businesses permit no more than three inner-circle firms to operate with sustained profitability in a mature market.

Outer-Circle Competitors Outer-circle players, once considered second-class citizens, are getting a fresh look. The traditional view that market share and return on investment were linearly correlated has been revisited in recent years. It now appears that the relationship is as shown in Figure 3.5.

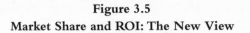

Figure 3.5
Market Share and ROI: The New View

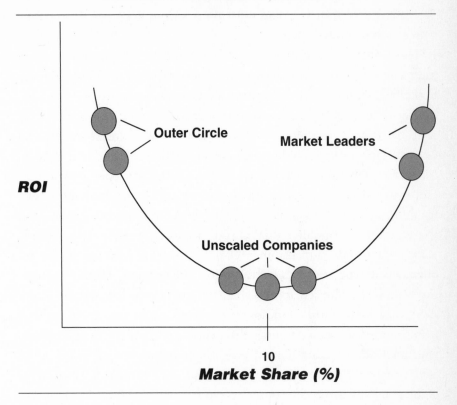

The typical industry contains any number of smaller firms with minimal market share that nonetheless report attractive returns on investment. Most industries have multiple small firms, often private, whose owners can do quite nicely indeed on a small revenue base.

A classic outer-circle firm has a very different profile from that of its larger neighbors. A pure outer-circle strategy involves a narrow line of products and services aimed at a highly specialized market need and customer base. An outer-circle firm will not invest in mass market branding, will not be vertically integrated, and will rely on third parties for substantial parts of its value chain. These firms may be technology or market specialists and may in particular possess deep expertise in a specific application or market niche.

The challenges for typical outer-circle firms are threefold. First, they must avoid the temptation to develop an organization and cost structure that resemble those of their larger rivals. Generally, niche players must be cautious about adding overhead costs—the outer circle does not support scale-based strategies. More fundamentally, organizational, financial, and operating formulas defined by the inner circle must be avoided at all costs. Niche players must resist accepting any element of the core competitor's business model. Sustained success as a niche player depends upon successful differentiation. Niche masters avoid emulating their larger rivals in any way, developing differentiated cost structures, technology platforms, value propositions, and customer relationships. They seek to identify and nurture distinct customer needs. Without differentiation, niche markets can readily be addressed and absorbed by inner circle competitors.

Second, under most conditions niche firms must resist the temptation to pursue growth opportunities that will draw them out of their profit zone and into the main field of play. Niche businesses generally should not be managed as growth companies. The best avenue for growth for a niche company is the development of other niches, using the same formula that worked in the home niche. Niche companies go wrong when they begin to act as if they have graduated to join the club, whose rules have been defined by the industry's inner circle. They fare far better when they pursue a *multiniche strategy*. Multiniche players create an interesting and rare subspecies in the market map. In the extreme case, niche mastery skills can be extended to multiple niche markets in the outer circle. Multi-niche champion Raychem operates over 2,000 outer-circle business units with average revenues under $5 million.

Third, outer-circle firms must find means for defending their niches. The best defense makes the market inaccessible and unpalatable to inner-circle and other competitors. Substantial entry investment requirements in unique local capabilities deter all competitors. Inner-circle competitors whose strategies stand on economies of scale should be particularly loathe to alter their standard business formulas. Successful niche players build high switching costs into unique solutions tailored to distinctive niche market needs. Larger competitors may probe but will generally pass on pursuing such niche markets.

Niche players exist largely at the mercy of their larger competitors. Only by obeying these rules can they be assured of ongoing success. With the right mindset, niche companies can be profitable, enduring players in the shadow of the mainstream.

Unscaled Competitors Another category of competitor doesn't have this luxury. Note that the middle section of the market share curve in Figure 3.5 shows a significant drop in return on investment (ROI). Firms in the midzone of this curve may actually be unprofitable, especially in market downturns; these are classic unscaled competitors. Such firms generically pursue the strategy and thereby possess the cost structure of an inner-circle competitor, without sufficient market share to support it. Unscaled companies are intensely vulnerable to cyclicality and industry downturns. Think of a firm like Gateway Computer as the PC market began to mature. Number five behind Dell, Compaq, IBM, and HP, Gateway's mainstream strategy performed fine during the rapid growth phase in the PC market. Its success cycle came to an abrupt end as slowing growth in PC shipments cramped unit sales, prices, and margins. Harnessed with the profile and cost structure of an inner-circle contender and without the gross margin to support it, Gateway found itself in no-man's-land. The HP-Compaq merger finalized the inner circle of three in the PC business and left Gateway standing even more clearly as an unscaled competitor. These companies essentially have two options: Either they can retreat to a profitable niche, or they can push on to profitability via growth in market share. Which of these strategic options is appropriate? The answer fundamentally depends on a single factor: the positions of other competitors in the business. If an unscaled competitor finds itself breathing the exhaust of three well-established inner circle competitors holding market shares of 35, 30, and 20 percent respectively, pushing ahead could be sheer folly.

Such firms normally possess but two choices in such circumstances: find a buyer for the company or retreat the business back to a profitable niche. The latter strategy is probably an impossible task for the existing management team. The team that landed the firm in its current dilemma would almost certainly be incapable of managing a retreat to profitability. Turnaround specialists may find such firms ideal candidates for their craft. The slipping unscaled competitor may be acquired and refocused into a profitable outer-circle niche player, or the firm may be acquired by one of the existing market leaders to consolidate a market position.

Now imagine another scenario. Let's say the firm is one of six companies, each with between 5 and 15 percent market share in a fast-growing industry. This firm should consider three generic strategy options. The first alternative is to push for market leadership as aggressively as possible. A merger or acquisition may be warranted, and the firm should certainly seek to position itself on Wall Street to secure the market value and financial resources needed to fund an aggressive growth-acquisition strategy. Second, the firm could position itself to be acquired by another industry player, thus ensuring that it would join the ultimate winning team in the market place. A timely merger with the emerging momentum leader could tip the industry crown into its hands. Third, this firm should actively examine breakthrough strategies to activate a tipping point and achieve market leadership.

The interesting variable under this scenario involves the intentions of the other five firms in the industry. If all six firms aggressively seek market leadership, yet no clear leader emerges, the horse race may continue until some tipping event occurs and shifts momentum to one or more of the competitors. If no firm can mount the necessary initiative to capture market leadership, an outside firm might acquire one of the players and provide the impetus to seize leadership. The winners are determined largely by three factors: capital, customers, and competitive strategy skills.

The unscaled firm is unstable and must move in one direction or the other. It must seek the shelter of a profitable niche or immediately gird itself to battle for inner-circle share and status.

The presence of unscaled firms in any industry should be of significant concern to an incumbent market leader because such firms inevitably destabilize their markets. If they embrace traditional attempts to gain market share, they can be dealt with directly; often, however, these firms embrace unusual strategies and break industry rules in their attempts to gain market share. Unscaled competitors are natural candidates to pursue breakthrough strategies. Perhaps a greater concern is that such firms may be acquired by a convergent or global competitor seeking to establish a foothold in the incumbent's marketplace.

MARKET DEFINITION

Understanding the competitive positions of key players in the target market is critical in shaping strategy. An even more fundamental issue facing any strategist is that of market scope and boundaries. The underlying question is the following: Is this business its own universe or is it part of a larger market structure? The answer to that question is rarely resolved solely by self-determination. The question fundamentally is, "Is our business (A) part of the mainstream of a larger industry, (B) a segment of the primary industry, (C) a niche in the larger industry, (D) a substitute for the industry, or (E) a truly independent business?" An honest answer to this question is absolutely central to shaping sound strategies. No strategy makes sense unless it first defines the scope of its setting. *Market def-*

Figure 3.6
Five Fundamental Market Positions

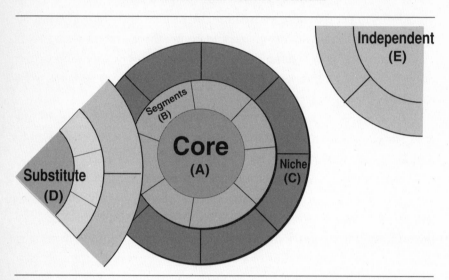

inition is a central skill of the strategist. Precise market definition depends on three simple factors:

- Supply side differentiation
- Demand side differentiation
- Competitive strategies

Put simply, businesses that do or can share common supply side platforms, serve common needs, and exhibit convergent strategies will become part of the same market structure. For example, are consumer telephony and business telephony distinct businesses or part of the same business? They both utilize the same network infrastructure, and—even better—at different times of the day! From the supply-side perspective, they are both addressable from the same platforms, and competitors who serve both groups will have a scale advantage over specialized carriers. Yet customer needs and sales and service models differ substantially, especially for large businesses. These demand-side variances suggest that large, distinct segments will appear in core telephony markets, leveraging common supply-side assets through differentiated solutions, marketing, sales, and service channels.

Niches and Segments

The distinction between a market segment and an industry niche is critical. A segment reflects a set of customers or a specific need that is related to the mainstream of a marketplace but is distinct in one or more demand dimensions. Nonetheless, a segment can be served from the mainstream supply and value chain of the core industry. In contrast, a niche in pure form involves a more distinct market need and customer set and involves a distinct supply and value chain. A true niche is differentiated from the mainstream of the core industry in both its supply and demand dimensions, whereas a segment is distinguished typically only by differentiation on the demand dimension as shown in Figure 3.7.

These distinctions are critical. They largely determine the ultimate map of any marketplace, determining which businesses will be integrated into the core and which will stand alone.

Effective strategies unambiguously and honestly address market scope. Many companies tend to define their markets too narrowly. Paging carriers might have once argued that theirs was a stand-alone business—until paging functions were incorporated into cell phones. Wireless operators might argue that they are part of a standalone business—until supercarriers incorporate wireless services into integrated service offerings. In the United States, integrated carriers already dominate the wireless market. The top five vendors are all affiliated with wireline-based carriers. All are in a position to integrate wireless offerings into a packaged set of services as soon as financial and regulatory disincentives diminish.

Integrated competitors can compete very effectively against shallow spe-

Figure 3.7
Market Space Definition

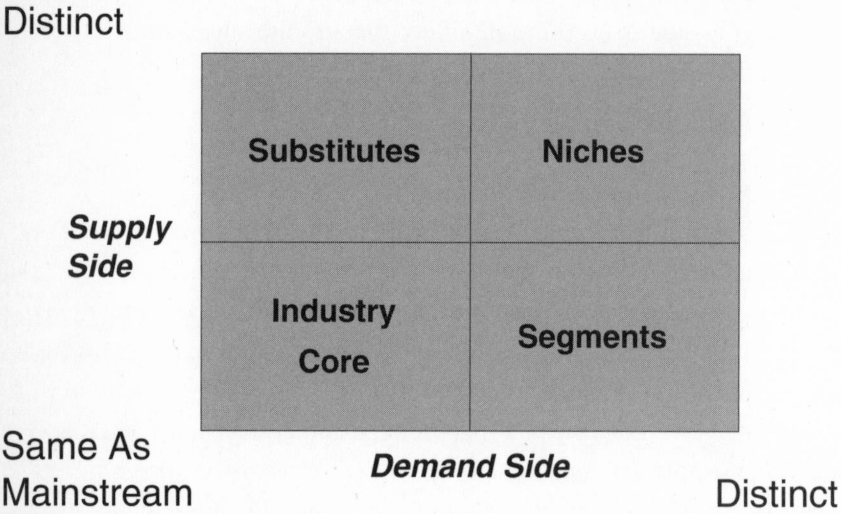

Distinct

Substitutes	**Niches**
Industry Core	**Segments**

Supply Side

Same As Mainstream   *Demand Side*

Distinct

cialists. In the most basic approach, they can offer the specialist's service free with purchase of a full package. Sophisticated inner-circle competitors will inevitably limit and shrink undifferentiated specialists. Specialists who believe they can defy this logic must possess powerful differentiating features, and that itself may not be enough to ensure success in the face of committed core competitors. The questions truly become the following: Can this business be annexed into the larger market? Will it become part of the profile of an inner-circle competitor in a larger industry? Focused pursuit of a narrow market becomes hazardous if the market in question will be subsumed into a broader business model.

Inner-circle competitors in any market will naturally probe all segments, outer-circle niches, and adjacent industries in search of business that can be addressed and assimilated from their supply platform. Niche and segment competitors will attempt to carve customers out of the core with tailored, differentiated offerings. That dynamic will exist to some extent in every industry. Here's an example of an inner-circle company entering a related market with initial extraordinary success.

The Niche Switch In the late 1980s, Allstate and Progressive coexisted peacefully in a fairly stable market. Allstate was a strong number-two inner-circle competitor in the standard auto insurance market, and Progressive had became the leader in the niche for substandard (high-risk) auto coverage. Business was good for Progressive, a "smart" company with earnings considerably above the average for auto insurers—indeed, things were so good that the company began to attract attention from its neighbors. Progressive's profitability in the nonstandard, high-risk segment of the market consistently outshone that of the rest of the auto insurance industry. Its underwriting profits averaged more than 800 basis points higher than the rest of the industry's in the 1980s.

Part of that difference stemmed from Progressive's lower-than-average sales costs. It had a small direct sales channel because most of its customers were referred to it by larger standard insurance companies. Allstate, which frequently referred clients rejected for standard coverage to Progressive, noticed that the Cleveland company's profits were substantially higher than its own. Seeing an opportunity, Allstate created a new unit to write substandard auto insurance policies. Rather than referring rejects to Progressive, Allstate's standard insurance group sent the "cream of the crap" down the hall to their new high-risk unit. In 1988, Allstate's underwriters began insuring the cream of their high-risk applicants, denying those profitable customers to Progressive. At the same time, Proposition 103 in 1988 in California rolled back auto insurance rates, forcing Progressive to curtail its booming business there. In just one year, Allstate displaced Progressive as the nation's leading seller of substandard auto coverage, proving that high-risk auto insurance was not a defensible niche but rather an addressable segment of the mainstream market. The ease and speed of Allstate's move into the high-risk market probably meant that segment players like Progressive could readily address the core market as well. That fact may be cold comfort for most segment specialists facing core competitors ten times or more larger than themselves. But Progressive took precisely this line of attack in reaction to Allstates's initiative.

Responding to the attack from its huge rival, Progressive targeted an area of marked weakness for Allstate—claims service. Stories about poor service at the hands of "Good Hands" claim adjusters were rife. CEO Peter Lewis decided to focus on claims settlement. As discussed earlier, Progressive placed mobile, communications-equipped claims adjusters in the field for quick support and claim settlement, often at the scene of an accident—on a 24/365 basis. The new service environment persuaded drivers that the company was on their side and lowered the total cost of claims.

Progressive's innovative Immediate Response Claims Settlement Service was designed to provide customers with a painless solution to car repair and payment that also drove big savings to the insurer. Taking advantage of its newfound cost advantage and service edge, Progressive broke out of its niche and stormed into the standard auto insurance market. Beginning in 1992, Progressive targeted drivers with good records in one state after another. It quickly became the largest U.S. personal auto insurer selling via independent agents. By the end of 1995, Progressive introduced standard auto insurance in every state where it operated.

1995 was also the year Sears, Roebuck and Company finished spinning off Allstate, which then set out to transform itself from a conglomerate to an operating company.[3] It got rid of noncore insurance operations and focused on auto, homeowner, and life coverage. In the auto business at least, the result was not impressive. From 1995 to 2000, Allstate's market share declined by about 10 percent. Progressive's, on the other hand, grew rapidly—at times leading the industry in premium gains—and it became the nation's fourth largest auto insurer, up from number 27 at the beginning of the decade. In 1997 alone, Progressive increased its net premiums written by $1 billion, a jump of nearly one third.

By 2001, in addition to affirming its brazen goal of becoming the top U.S. auto insurer, Progressive had begun to enter the adjacent home insurance market. Still number two among home insurers, albeit with a declining share, Allstate was about to face the pesky Progressive in yet another core market. Would the home insurance market be addressable from Progressive's auto insurance base? Would its breakthrough platforms and strategy transfer to this adjacent space? Allstate's foray into Progressive's segment had triggered a series of forces that would reshape much of the insurance sector. Progressive's innovative response to invasion by a larger inner-circle competitor provides a classic example of the breakout niche strategy. A number of the most successful insurgents in our research sample are breakout niche players—established, secondary competitors who use innovation and industry experience to seize market leadership.

Convergent Competitors

In many industries, the most formidable competitive force comes from adjacent markets. Of course, for many firms, the biggest opportunity lies in adjacent markets. The term *convergence* has been widely used to describe the integration of previously independent market sectors. The term is misleading in that there is nothing graceful or fluid about this exercise; it resembles far more the embrace of opposing armies. The one certainty of this process is that there will be fatalities among the participants. Whether it be regional businesses that are globalizing or related market sectors that are integrating, the effect of convergence—or collision—is identical. In either case, once-distinct industry structures merge to form a new order as barriers that once kept sets of companies from competing diminish or disappear. A classic example of convergence, in the form of globalization, occurred in the tire industry over the past several decades.

Rolling Globalization In the early 1980s, the world tire industry was organized primarily into distinct regional markets. Goodyear, Firestone, and Goodrich dominated the North American market, with second-tier players Uniroyal and General in tow. In Europe, a series of national players dominated their home markets and were rapidly consolidating to form a regional European market. Michelin, Continental, Dunlop, and Pirelli were the primary players. Michelin had somewhat reluctantly acquired Kleber Colombes to keep that company in French hands, while Continental had acquired Uniroyal Europe. Japanese manufacturers Bridgestone, Yokohama, Sumitomo, and Asahi dominated the Asian region. Asian markets often stretch the rule of three because of the semi-captive *keiretsu/chaebol/hong* industrial structures that support participants in each major industry sector. Nonetheless, the Japanese market was dominated by the three largest players to an extent comparable to or greater than what was seen in the United States or Europe.

As the 1980s began, market structures in the United States and Japan were remarkably stable and had changed little in over a decade. Europe was experiencing some change due to the shift from national to regional markets, yet the major players had not changed significantly. Over the next decade, all this would change dramatically.

The process of globalization was triggered by several key events. The introduction of the radial tire into North American markets by Michelin was a key catalyst. Michelin had largely completed the radialization of the European market by the early 1970s and had shifted its focus to the rest of the world. American tire markers had recently invested in a new generation of production capacity for bias-belted tires and were rationally reluctant to displace those investments. The U.S. tire industry had also succumbed to a tight pattern of oligopolistic competitive behavior. All of the players had learned that it was unwise to launch competitive initiatives in the face of certain response by their peers. Tires exhibit low price elasticity: Price reductions are not met by a proportionate increase in unit demand. Over the years, industry players had learned that pricing initiatives designed to increase market share would be matched by competitors, resulting in lower prices and margins for everyone without any increase in volume or shifts in market share. Promotion initiatives, channel incentives, or other marketing thrusts would lead to the same result. The industry had stabilized and was unprepared for the destructive impact of new technology and competition.

U.S. tire makers did little to address the arrival of the radial tire. At the same time, Japanese producers were rapidly expanding their penetration into the low end of the U.S. market, selling tires at less than half the average price of U.S.-made tires.[4] Again, given price inelasticity, U.S. tire makers were loathe to compete head-to-head on that front. Meeting either threat head-on—radials at the high end or Japanese competitors at the low end—would ultimately lead to reduced profitability. Although radial tires offered higher unit prices, they required substantial new capital investment, and their much longer tire life resulted in reduced unit volumes. U.S. tire makers were in a difficult spot. Consequently, the U.S. industry response to these new realities was not forceful. Meanwhile, European and Japanese competitors saw nothing but market opportunity in the United States. From 1966 to 1972, imports had risen from 1 percent to 5.6 percent of the U.S. replacement tire market and were still growing.

Michelin set distribution agreements with Sears and others and developed meaningful inroads into the market. By 1978, Michelin was operating three tire plants in the United States and two in Canada and had captured fully 9 percent of the U.S. automotive replacement market—and that did not even count the Michelin-made radials that were being sold by Sears, Roebuck and Company under the store brand.[5] With share eroding and driven by industry leader Goodyear, the U.S. industry ultimately fought its way out of the bunker mentality it had developed. By the late 1970s, Goodyear had made a major commitment to radial tire production capacity—a $2 billion investment that signaled a shift in the industry's evolution. It had some catching up to do—by 1978, Michelin had captured more than 30 percent of the total truck tire market. Bridgestone also had 10 percent of the replacement truck tire market by that time. Goodyear CEO Chuck Pilliod often reminded his executives, "Don't waste your time looking over your shoulders at the Firestones, Uniroyals, and Goodriches. Look at the French and the Japanese."

The other makers followed Goodyear into radials. As the seventies drew to a close, the pressure of massive capital investment required to build radial tire capacity as well as reduced margins and increased advertising expense began to take their toll on other participants. Industry profitability shrank dramatically. In 1978, Uniroyal had to sell its best plants and seek wage concessions from employees. In 1980, Firestone closed five U.S. plants, Goodrich barely eked out a profit and gave up selling tires to Detroit automakers, and General Tire was using profits from its broadcast subsidiary to offset tire losses.[6] In this capital-intensive, low-margin industry, the pressures of consolidation were particularly acute and the results inevitable:

1981: Firestone sells its Nashville truck tire plant to Bridgestone, and the companies begin a broader conversation.

1983: Dunlop sells its European tire operations to Sumitomo of Japan.

1984: Sumitomo buys Dunlop's North American tire operations.

1986: Uniroyal and Goodrich merge their tire operations.

1987: General Tire is acquired by Germany's Continental Tire. Firestone is acquired by Japan's Bridgestone in the largest Japanese takeover of an American company to date.

1988: Pirelli buys Armstrong Tire. After operating jointly with Uniroyal for several years, Goodrich exits the business and focuses its efforts in the chemical business.

1990: Michelin buys the Uniroyal/Goodrich tire operation for $1.5 billion. Uniroyal shifts its efforts to the chemical industry.

By 1990, Goodyear, with about 30 percent of the U.S. passenger tire market, and niche player Cooper Tire were the only original U.S. tire makers left. It took a bit longer for the process of consolidation to play out in Japan. It wasn't until 1999 that Goodyear and Sumitomo, by that time the world's third and fifth biggest tire makers, announced a global "alliance" (though there was no doubt about who was the senior partner) that would vault them into first place with 22 percent of the world market versus Bridgestone and Michelin, each with 18 percent.[7] Michelin was denying rumors that it planned to acquire Yokohama.

At that point in time, the big three tire makers accounted for roughly 60 percent of the industry's total world market, and a new order had been achieved as seen in Figure 3.8. The rule of three was now very much in effect. The next-largest competitor, Continental, held a market share of less than 10 percent. Although Continental appeared to be unscaled, its business model is essentially that of a multiniche competitor and its sales derived from a series of specific markets and segments that had some degree of defensibility. Much of its unit volume came from third-world countries where it enjoyed solid political barriers and protected markets, including India and Egypt. In addition, it had close relationships with German carmakers and—through the acquisition of ITT's automotive parts business—had begun to shift towards the production of integrated tire, wheel, and brake assemblies, hinting at a potential new convergence cycle for the tire industry.

Notably, at the end of the globalization cycle, one European, one American, and one Japanese competitor dominated the tire industry structure. The process of globalization had weeded out all but the single strongest player in each of these regions. Is this new structure stable? The inner-circle competitors have come to know each other well, and a new

Figure 3.8
The Tire Industry Globalization Process

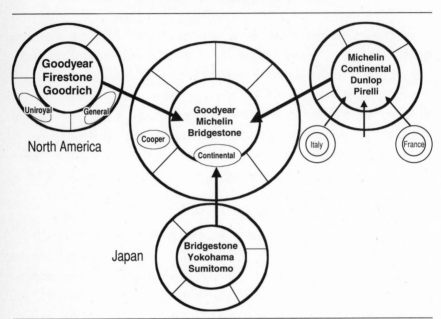

set of rules have been established for industry conduct. Two decades of dramatic and dynamic globalization have led to the creation of a classic and seemingly stable market structure, but a dozen noted companies are no more. The winners, Goodyear, Michelin, and Bridgestone, can enjoy their victory—until the next breakthrough triggers a new transformation cycle.

The Strategist's Task The tire industry was dominated for decades by the dynamics of globalization. Any strategy in this industry had to begin with a clear understanding of that process. Industry convergence involves a similar process, as once-distinct businesses merge to form a new, larger sector. That dynamic dominates the telecom sector today as local and long distance markets collide, with predictable results. Wireless and wire-line communication may also converge, and cable TV and telecom already exhibit extensive overlap. In such settings, strategists must take into account shifts in market boundaries in shaping their plans. In converging markets, a key focal point for strategic change will be the company's profile. Transformation strategies ranging from constructing an expanded inner-circle profile in a global business, to shrinking into a defensible niche with a specialists' profile, should be considered.

Here's one more key point: The convergence and integration of markets can be seen as a Darwinian or Hegelian contest between rival technologies, products, business models, and business communities. It is a process that results in conquest, synthesis, or differentiation. That point of view is relevant and powerful, but convergence is ultimately about competition between corporations—not technologies, products, or other business elements. Free will is fundamental on this planet. Effective competitors are able to detach themselves from specific technologies or other business elements to focus on the broader challenge of mastering a converging market. The primary question is not what products or technologies will win; rather, it is which companies will ultimately come to secure customers and market share and define the profile of an inner-circle competitor in the relevant market.

Convergence specifically forces dramatic changes in a firm's profile and position. Firms who were inner-circle players in a predecessor market become marginalized and must either scale up to the new standard or shift to a niche profile. That means more than a shift in focus—it requires a transformation at the core from an inner-circle profile and identity to that of a niche player. Mergers or dramatic investments may be part of that exercise, but these steps alone will not complete the necessary transformation to a new profile and competitive position.

Convergence forces firms to transform themselves, one way or another. Breakthrough strategies are an appropriate response to, or (trigger for) convergence and other market shifts but do not embark on the path to breakthrough without insight and consideration. Shaping strategy in any setting requires careful examination of market context and competitive dynamics. Strategy formulation begins with the following core skills:

- *Market mapping*—defining the scope and boundaries of primary and related businesses
- *Market research*—grasping key customer realities and opportunities
- *Competitor classification and assessment*—recognizing and evaluating the generic positions and players in the marketplace
- *Setting aspirations*—defining profit and position goals
- *Strategic role selection*—picking and playing the available role in a given market or finding a market which will support a preferred role
- *Securing the strategic position*—defending a profitable niche or protecting a market leadership position
- *Designing strategy drivers*—perfecting performance (process) and profile engines to achieve goals
- *Defining the preferred profile*—perfecting the product portfolio, market coverage, value chain, and economic structure for your strategy
- *Achieving performance targets*—reengineering processes, technology, and people to achieve operating performance targets
- *Maximizing market space*—developing or conquering additional market opportunities adjacent to the core market that can be readily addressed and assimilated

These skills are generic to any strategy formulation effort. Our core concern here is to determine whether a breakthrough strategy fits your current, evolving situation. Begin with an assessment of your business environment. Identify your position relative to existing key players and key market trends. Aggressively, but realistically, set your aspirations. Make an informed decision before selecting and shaping a breakthrough strategy.

As you shape your strategy, especially if it is of breakthrough proportions, carefully consider market and competitive realities, as well as your own corporate identity; define your aspirations in terms of competitive position and financial performance; identify the key performance and profile drivers for success; and integrate the above into a focused strategy. Next, we'll talk about how to turn that strategy into results.

NOTES

1. Katherine Hobson, "Kohl's Promises Big Things as Big Boxes Push into Northeast," TheStreet.com, March 2, 2000.

2. Jagdish Sheth and Rajendra Sisodia, *The Rule of Three,* The Free Press, 2002.

3. Barbara Bowers, "Putting on the Squeeze," *Best's Review,* Property/Casualty Edition, August 1999, p. 53.

4. David Harkleroad, "Pneumatiques Michelin 1B." In *Managing the Global Corporation: Case Studies in Strategy and Management,* William Davidson and Jose de la Torre, editors. New York: McGraw Hill, 1989.

5. *Managing the Global Corporation,* op. cit.

6. Ron Shinn, "Through the Wringer at Goodyear," *New York Times,* May 24, 1981, p. 3.

7. "Sumitomo Rubber, Goodyear Sign Global Alliance Deal," *Japan Weekly Monitor,* Feb. 8, 1999.

CHAPTER 4

CHAMPIONS OF BREAKTHROUGH

BREAKTHROUGH STRATEGIES begin with outrageous objectives. Those objectives may focus on any or all of the four key strategy dimensions: profit (including all financial targets), operating performance (including processes), profile, and position. These goals may be expressed in statements such as the following:

- *Position:* We will become the market leader in an industry.
- *Profit:* We will achieve revenue of x profit of y, or market value of z.
- *Performance:* We will deliver the best customer service in the market.
- *Performance:* We will become the industry's cost leader.
- *Performance:* We will achieve Six Sigma quality standards.
- *Profile:* We will become the end-to-end provider of a full line of integrated services.
- *Profile:* We will develop a leadership position in global markets.

After an organization embraces a goal of this nature, everything else can begin to come into focus around a strategy to achieve the goal. Regardless of the goal, operating performance and profile initiatives provide the key engines for reaching it. Gains in competitive position and financial results can only come from improvement in these key drivers. For most companies, it will be very difficult to significantly alter financial performance and virtually impossible to improve competitive position without meaningful change in performance, profile, or both. Unless you are enjoying the momentum of a previous innovation or benefiting from particularly fortuitous market trends beyond your control, gains are unlikely to occur without innovation in these key dimensions.

The key variables in a company's profile are its product/market/channel map, its value chain, and its organizational model. Profile initiatives include all new product or service activity, channel innovations, market participation and coverage, value chain/vertical integration initiatives, organizational change, and acquisitions that affect any of the aforementioned items. Profile initiatives can be quite powerful, but few breakthrough companies focus exclusively on profile innovation as the key driver of their strategy.

Toyota Motors, one of the most successful companies in our study, achieved remarkable success with its Lexus line. Lexus was a profile innovation that leveraged a new product introduction to dramatically expand the company's profile into the upscale, luxury auto market segment. However, the success of that breakthrough was built upon Toyota's manufacturing system, including its lean manufacturing, Just-in-Time (JIT) inventory, Kaizen continuous improvement methodology, design for manufacturability techniques, and more: all powerful operating performance innovations. For firms in service industries, process innovation and new service introduction are even more intimately linked. Radical innovation in operating performance appears to be the single best driver of breakthroughs in financial performance, competitive position, and expanded corporate profile.

DELL'S PERFORMANCE ENGINE

Operating performance or process innovations play a central role in most breakthroughs. Dell Computer provides a powerful example of how innovations in operating performance carried a marginal competitor to market leadership. Dell Computer was an undistinguished face in the PC crowd during the first half of the 1990s. Despite strong sales growth, Dell only held about 3 percent of the market for personal computer systems in 1994, and it lost $36 million that year. At the midpoint of the 1990s, Dell was busy consolidating operations, writing off assets, and booking employee severance payments.

Five years later, Dell became the leading PC vendor in the United States, followed by Compaq, Hewlett-Packard, Gateway, and IBM. In 2001, Dell became the *worldwide* market leader in PC sales. Delegated briefly to the number two spot following the HP-Compaq merger, Dell reclaimed the mantle of market leadership in less than one month. In the workstation market, Dell also achieved worldwide market leadership. In PC servers, Dell is second among the top four vendors, who control nearly three fourths of revenues in a rapidly consolidating market. For small businesses, it was the most widely purchased brand of desktop and notebook PC, with 19 and 24 percent market share, respectively.[1]

All of Dell's success sprang from breakthrough innovation centered in core operations. Dell tightly integrated its customer service, supply chain, production scheduling, and fulfillment functions into its direct sales front end, improving operating efficiency, cycle times, and customer service. It converted cost savings into competitive pricing that generated both growing market share and profitability.

Dell was a pioneer in PC telemarketing, but the real breakthrough occurred in 1995 when founder Michael Dell forced the company to fully focus on direct sales over the Internet via its Dell.com website. Sales over the Internet reached $50 million per day, and half of Dell's sales were booked online by the end of the decade. Dell's breakthrough was more than a sales channel innovation. It was the first to embrace mass customization of PCs. Every customized computer system was built to order on a just-in-time basis and shipped within days, slicing weeks off the company's inventory.[2] Dell was the first company to perfect a now-generic breakthrough strategy that combines mass customization; customer-specific product design; just-in-time supply chain solutions; and rapid, remote fulfillment and service. The result was typical of successful breakthroughs—rapid sales growth and rising margins. One dimension of Dell's performance breakthrough appears in Figure 4.1, which shows the dramatic reductions in inventory it achieves with its new business model.

Dell's stock was the top performer in the S&P 500 during the 1990s. It ranked number three on the Fortune list of most admired companies in 2000. Dell had joined—if not passed—such computer industry leaders as IBM and HP in the rarified air of high-profile brands and mega-

Figure 4.1
Dell's Days Sales in Inventory

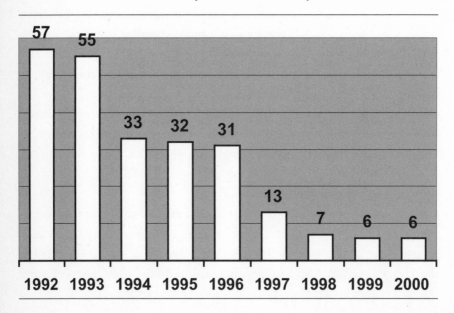

Table 4.1
Dell's Market Momentum

	2002		2001	
	Revenue	*Profit*	*Revenue*	*Profit*
Dell	$35.4B	$2.1B	$31.9B	$1.2B
Gateway	$4.2B	($309M)	$6.1B	($1.3B)

market caps. It was extremely well positioned to maintain its market leadership as industry consolidation began to constrict the PC industry in 2001, and the rule of three began to kick in. As the PC market tightened, Dell began to pull away from its peers in the PC business. For 2002, Dell reported healthy sales growth and a profits increase of 70 percent to $2.1 billion, while Gateway experienced declining revenues and a loss of $309 million (see Table 4.1). Dell's market momentum, which originated in its breakthrough business model, continues to carry it to new heights. In addition to its core PC business, Dell's server sales grew sharply in 2002, and its data storage business grew at 50 percent per quarter during the year.

Dell's success shows how a small, second-tier competitor can move out of the shadow of much larger rivals and seize market leadership by embracing a breakthrough strategy. Its strategy started with a powerful performance innovation that drove dramatic gains in profits and financial value, competitive position, and profile. Dell's profile continues to expand as it moves aggressively into workstations, servers, data storage, and beyond.

Let's look at another Texas-based upstart that used operating performance to drive it from obscurity to center stage. No industry has suffered so much in recent years as the airline industry. Yet one carrier continues to fly high, a former subregional carrier turned national insurgent. Today, Southwest Airlines' market value is greater than Delta's, greater than Northwest's, even greater then American's—combined.

Figure 4.2
Airlines' Market Share vs. Value

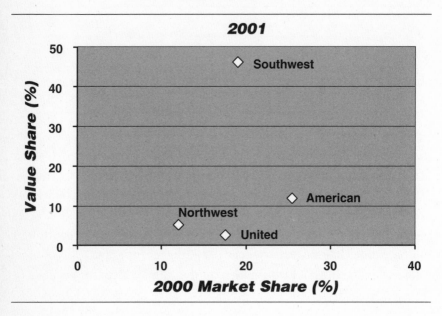

Perhaps it seems unusual to consider a company with a $10 billion market cap an "insurgent" when the leading incumbent has a market cap of less than $1 billion. Yet that's just the way the domestic airline industry seems to treat Southwest Airlines a quarter century after its founding and long after it changed the rules in the airline business. With about 10 percent of industry revenues, Southwest captures more than half of total industry value (see Figure 4.2).

Southwest Airlines is aptly named, as insurgents emerge from the southwest corner of the value/market share map and take flight. Southwest Airlines fought for its very survival for years before it found clear skies. Often, overnight successes occur only after long, difficult journeys.

In 1994, after 20 years of often-precarious existence, Southwest Airlines was in market position number eight, with only a 3.3 percent share. It was making money but was locked out of three of the four U.S. computer airline reservations systems. United, Continental Airlines, and Delta Airlines had blackballed Southwest in order to protect their routes. Southwest responded by using its own 800 number and later its own website to sell seats, using a ticketless and seatless (no assigned seats) model. Both were in keeping with its no-frills service model. The major carriers periodically matched Southwest's low fares, although typically for a "limited number of seats" in competing markets and with a 21-day advance purchase restriction. However, the other major carriers saw such low fares as temporary price wars, not a paradigm shift. What, after all, had become of People Express, the prototypical discount upstart, or other insurgents such as New York Air? The incumbents had seen this act before, and those upstarts were runway kill. For the new breed of discounters, was it not therefore only a matter of time?

High-cost majors like Northwest saw the industry in terms of two tiers. In one tier, from primary hubs, they served the well-heeled-business travelers and folks who wanted traditional service and didn't like scrambling for seats. In the other tier, the discounters flew budget-minded folk from one out-of-the-way burg to another in low-class planes with lousy quality, safety, and service.

Southwest, however, saw the world in a different way. It saw itself as a short-haul, high-frequency airline. Because it saw cars, trains, and buses as its primary substitutes, it had built its cost structure to compete with them. Its business model had been built not on "this week only" or seasonal specials, but on low fares forever. In keeping with such a lean cost structure, Southwest founder and boss Herb Kelleher didn't draw down a lot of long-term debt to buy new airplanes—he paid mostly cash. He paid his pilots three-fourths what the big airlines paid theirs. Those pilots flew one third more hours and occasionally pitched in to clean the cabins. (Even so, the airline has been a regular on Fortune Magazine's annual list of best companies to work for.) In 1995, Southwest signed a 10-

year pay deal with their pilots, eliminating one aspect of an issue that has been a constant headache for the majors. In 1996, it cost Southwest just 7.5 cents to fly one seat one mile, well below the industry average of about 9 cents.

What else did Southwest do? It flew only Boeing 737s, which saved money on scheduling, training, and maintenance. It kept its airplanes in the air more hours per day, making better use of its capital. It turned around its planes at the gate in a fraction of industry standards, gaining extra flights each day in the process. I don't think I've ever waited more than 10 seconds for the front door to open after a Southwest flight docks at the gate, whereas lengthy disembarking delays are all too common on other airlines. It also avoided the entire expense and bother of providing hot airline meals—one lesson the other "premium" airlines appear to have learned.

The major carriers tried to protect their market by limiting Southwest's access to gates they controlled at important airports. But Southwest would just outflank the majors by initiating service at smaller airports like Chicago's Midway Airport and in places like Albany, NY and Providence, RI. Southwest didn't need to run specials; it just needed to run more flights. Every year, Southwest added cities like Boise, ID and Manchester, NY to its service and new nonstop routes like Baltimore-Oakland and Kansas City-Seattle. As it sought airports away from the expensive hubs, soon smaller cities eagerly recruited Southwest to serve their communities. And just as often, the major airlines would quickly dump those routes from their schedules. In 1999, 171 U.S. cities asked Southwest Airlines to provide flights at their airports.

Southwest Airlines' market cap gives it the option to acquire any of the old-guard airlines, yet it is highly unlikely that it would ever do so. It is growing organically at an impressive pace and will likely continue to hold the leader's share of market value in the domestic airline industry. Now shifting from its regional short-haul profile to a national, long-haul model,

Southwest is redefining the inner circle of the airline industry. It is in effect moving its niche position into the core of the market, transforming the mainstream in the process. That same process is occurring in the financial service sector.

A SLOW, SPECTACULAR MARCH TO MARKET LEADERSHIP

In December 1998, Charles Schwab's market capitalization first surpassed that of Merrill Lynch, $25.5 billion to $25.4 billion. Merrill had $11.4 billion in equity versus Schwab's $1.9 billion; $1.5 trillion in customer assets versus Schwab's $600 billion; and 66,000 employees versus Schwab's 17,400.[3] But Schwab was worth more to investors. To the uninformed it might have appeared to be an overnight e-commerce success, but Schwab's success was the result of decades of often frustrating efforts to achieve a breakthrough in the brokerage business (see Figure 4.3).

Charles (Chuck) Schwab started his business in 1971 with a mission of providing individual investors with low-cost, high-quality service minus selling pressure. Seeing a new market materializing for cost-sensitive customers, Schwab cut its fees and—along with several other upstarts—got the discount brokerage industry on its way.

Schwab went beyond cutting rates; he concentrated on quick and efficient execution of customer orders. Bucking the standard 35–40 percent commission the big houses paid brokers on trading fees, he paid his brokers a fixed salary plus a bonus based on company performance. A decade after its founding, Schwab was king of the bargain-basement brokers, with 29 offices, 160,000 clients, and $40 million in revenues. Schwab was at the head of the class of some 50 discount brokers who together garnered 10 percent of all retail brokerage transactions and 5 percent of commissions.[4] Merrill execs saw the cut-rate market as nearly

Figure 4.3
Battle of the Brokerage Houses

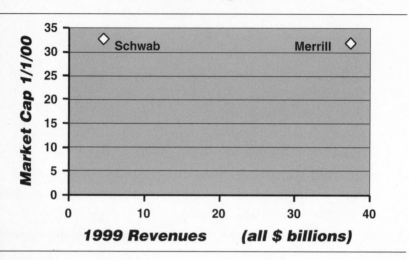

saturated,[5] but Chuck Schwab believed that "discounters are a staying force and we'll take an increasing share of the market as investors become more sophisticated."[6]

A person who wished to trade 300 shares of a $35 stock in 1983 would have paid Merrill Lynch $191.69 and Schwab only $88.50. A number of discount competitors were in the same ballpark, but Schwab differentiated itself by pioneering 24-hour service, offering no-load mutual fund supermarkets and establishing automated, self-service trading operations.

Big bets on information technology were an essential aspect of Schwab's strategy from the beginning. In the 1970s, for example, the company spent a year's worth of revenue on an IBM mainframe to automate trading and reporting. Such investments in back-office technology paid off as Schwab service reps confirmed orders in 90 seconds and handled most trades in a paperless fashion. By 1989, Schwab could accept automated trades via push-button telephones and personal computers.

Schwab's aggressive and innovative approach to technology led to numerous failures over the years. In retrospect, Chuck Schwab calls them "noble failures," flawed attempts to achieve a vision that endured until a sustainable breakthrough was achieved. Noble failures have been something of a tradition at Schwab since the company's founding. Many of them have been attempts to use the latest technology to provide Schwab customers with the most timely financial and market information. Among them were the following:

- *Pocketerm*—a handheld device that was supposed to act like a portable stock quotation machine. The gadget never worked properly and was dropped.
- *Schwabline*—an electromechanical desktop device for printing out a customer's portfolio value. "Unfortunately the device was electromechanical with lots of springs and things inside, so there were all kinds of opportunities for it to break down," Schwab recalls.
- *Financial Independence*—this software product enabled users to manage all personal financial information but required computer savvy and did not permit account management.
- *The Equalizer*—Schwab's attempt to let customers issue orders from their desktop computers via modem. Once again, users needed computer knowledge and the product was buggy, but it later appeared in a Windows version as StreetSmart.[7]

This undying interest in using technology to help customers manage their investments and do business more conveniently led directly to Chuck Schwab's early interest in the Internet. After seeing a demonstration in the early 1990s, he said, "When I saw what could be done, I was flabbergasted." The first fruit of the company's Internet push was e.Schwab, an independent division focused on the web. In 1995, it also began offering trading through America Online (AOL), thus gaining access to the 7 million people who were then using AOL. Sensing a breakthrough, the firm expanded its online capacity eightfold to enable 80,000 simultaneous log-ons.

Growth followed quickly. Online accounts leaped to 2.2 million in 1996, exactly 40 percent of total accounts.[8] Furthermore, by offering sophisticated online services and tools to independent investment managers, the company opened up an important indirect channel. Assets in wholesale accounts from investment managers reached $146 billion by 2000. Schwab, king of discounters, thus redefined itself as a full-service click-and-mortar brokerage house.

As the twentieth century came to a close, a flood of investor dollars inundated the nation's stockbrokers. Customer assets at the top four brokerage firms/mutual funds companies—Merrill Lynch, Vanguard, Fidelity Investments, and Schwab—equaled more than half of all the deposits in U.S. banks.[9] More than 1.8 million new online trading accounts were opened in the last quarter of 1999. Online brokerage account assets rose more than one third, passing $900 billion—a number equal to more than 21 percent of bank deposits—and Schwab had the lion's share of that market.

At the turn of the millennium, Schwab, a brokerage firm that had pioneered discount brokerage a quarter century earlier, was the number one online stockbroker with a 22 percent market share and $350 billion in assets from online investors.[10] Achieving substantiated leadership in the next generation business model is the surest way to win Wall Street recognition and valuation as an emerging market leader.

As 2000 began, Schwab customer assets totaled $725 billion, up 48 percent from 1998. With 325 branch offices buttressed by Internet access, it had opened more than 1 million new accounts for the second consecutive year, bringing its grand total to 6.6 million accounts. With its bricks-and-clicks combination of frontline human and online customer service, Schwab was the big winner in the booming brokerage decade of the 1990s.

Do Look Down

Schwab's momentum slowed sharply in the down beat early years of the new decade. Though it remains market leader in online trading, it faces a much more difficult environment. An emerging market leader primarily and appropriately focuses upward and forward; its energies targeted on the incumbents it intends to displace. But just as incumbents must focus on disruptive insurgents, emerging market leaders must also occasionally look over their shoulders at next-generation competitors. Schwab holds a less than 5 percent market share in the total brokerage services business, despite a compound growth rate of 40 percent in customer assets during the 1990s. Its primary challenge over the next decade will be to achieve a place among the leaders in the converging brokerage and investment banking industry, yet it must also remain cognizant of a set of new-age competitors intent on capturing value and market share at its expense. Pure-play Internet trading companies—E*Trade, Ameritrade, and others—have already achieved recognition from investors in both physical and financial markets, as shown in Figure 4.4.

In addition to web startups, Schwab has to watch out for the more innovative Wall Street incumbents' efforts to capture online market share and capitalization as well. In the home lending market, agile incumbents successfully recaptured market leadership from insurgent Countrywide. Could the same result occur in the brokerage business? Look at the online offshoot of Donaldson, Lufkin, Jenrette (DLJ), now part of Credit Suisse First Boston. Other established players may also forcefully embrace online trading or change the game to their advantage in other ways.

Schwab must also concern itself with emerging competitors. Like Southwest Airlines, Schwab has enjoyed a substantial advantage over established incumbents by offering services at less than half the cost of its traditional rivals. Some of Schwab's new competitors have turned the tables and offer trading services at a small fraction of Schwab's prices. Schwab typically charges $29 for an online trade ($14.95 for frequent

Figure 4.4
Leading Online Brokers:
Market Share and Value Share

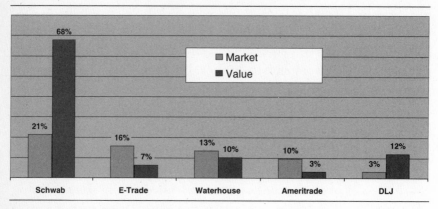

Sources: U.S. Bancorp Piper Jaffray, Yahoo!

traders); its emerging competitors' prices fall in the $10 range, and several have begun offering commission-free Internet trades. Among those are Ameritrade and FinancialCafe.com, which both see margin loans, trading spreads, advertising, credit cards, and so on as alternate revenue sources. Schwab now finds itself in the sights of a set of aggressive and disruptive new wave insurgents.

The Ides of March

The march from successful market launch to market leadership resembles a high-wire act. Any slip can be disastrous. At the midpoint of this passage, insurgent companies are likely to face concerted responses from established competitors as well as disruptive competition from next-generation contenders. Schwab provides an interesting response to this problem.

Schwab continues to expand its range of services and offerings. The acquisition of US Trust in 2000 positions Schwab to compete ever more effectively with both its established and insurgent competitors. The retail brokerage industry has become the preserve of investment banks, as one after another brokerage house has been gobbled up by the likes of Salomon (Smith Barney), Morgan Stanley (Dean Witter), and UBS (Paine Webber). US Trust allows Schwab to provide "white shoe" investment and private banking services to upscale clientele, in the heart of the investment bankers' market.

Schwab is positioning itself to be a full-line financial services house able to compete across the board with established players. At the same time, Schwab's advertising campaigns recently have begun to focus on emerging competitors. One ad shows a telephone dangling from a cord in an empty data center, with computer tapes spinning in the background. The customer on the phone expresses a concern about a particular holding and asks whether he should sell or hold the specific security. As the phone dangles, the customer says, "Take your time—I'm in no hurry." After a pregnant pause and more whirling of tapes, the customer says, "Hello? Hello? Is anyone there?" Schwab is positioning itself as a full-line service provider relative to the pure online trading companies while it moves upmarket into financial services and investment banking. Schwab's principal engine of growth will continue to be online trading, which now accounts for over 75 percent of all Schwab transactions. It is attempting to differentiate itself from less expensive Internet offerings through a full profile of product and professional service offerings. That full-line strategy moves it closer to core competitor Merrill Lynch's profile, setting up a classic confrontation between an East Coast established incumbent and a West Coast insurgent. Giant Merrill Lynch has shown signs of awakening to this battle, and Schwab will have its hands full on at least two fronts, facing an aroused incumbent and pesky new-wave insurgents. No longer an insurgent and not yet a market champion, Schwab's midmarch years promise to be more challenging than its glorious decade of the 1990s.

INCUMBENTS VERSUS INSURGENTS

Battles between insurgents and incumbents for market leadership often involve high drama. Insurgents generally can only win these wars if they possess a powerful breakthrough strategy that delivers real results in the marketplace. Here's an example of such a competition for leadership in the mortgage lending business. In one corner was First Nationwide Bank, its bold name indicating the extent of its ambitions. In the opposite corner was another California-based lender, an insurgent with equally grand ambitions: Countrywide Credit Industries. Both firms set out at precisely the same time in pursuit of the same objective—but there the similarity ends.

A hundred years after its founding, First Nationwide had grown into one of the ten largest savings and loans in the United States, with more than $11 billion in assets and branches in its home state, Florida, New York and Hawaii. While many S and Ls were operating in the red in the late 1980s, First Nationwide Bank was profitable. First Nationwide had purchased sickly S and Ls in Florida and New York, making it one of the first such firms in U.S. history to operate outside its home state. Targeting middle-income home buyers in particular, First Nationwide had already embarked on a plan to open more than 100 branch offices in Kmart stores around the United States, including thirty-eight in the "mortgage central" state of California.

Exactly a century after it opened for business, First Nationwide was acquired in 1985 by Ford Motor Company for $493 million. For the Michigan carmaker, this represented a major move in its plan to diversify into financial services. Competitor Chrysler had recently bought Bank of America's consumer finance operation, and General Motors (GM) had purchased the Colonial group of mortgage bankers. In some quarters, Ford was hailed as a visionary for its action. Like its sister automakers, cash-rich Ford bought its new S and L, intending for First Nationwide to grow and provide a countercyclical source of profits to the core automotive business. Indeed, the objective was to build First Nationwide into a financial giant and market leader in mortgage lending.

National Ambitions Won and Lost

Unlike GM and Chrysler, however, Ford had made its acquisition in the highly regulated S and L industry—an industry whose problems were only just beginning. With Ford's approval, incumbent First Nationwide CEO Anthony Frank (who later became U.S. Postmaster General) launched an ambitious, $500 million S and L buying program. Intending to multiply its mortgage business and become a truly nationwide thrift, First Nationwide purchased insolvent and troubled savings and loans in 14 states and unsuccessfully attempted to take over several others. Its assets rose from $12 billion in 1985 to more than $30 billion over the next decade.

As interest rates dropped in 1986 and the real estate market began picking up speed, however, potential First Nationwide mortgage clients weren't praising the thrift for its acquisitional prowess. They were complaining about lengthy delays in processing their loan applications. One First Nationwide loan agent told the San Diego Union-Tribune, "We're running two months (for a loan turnaround) and we're told to quote three." Computers would automatically knock out form letters explaining the long delays. Those customers who didn't want to buy a house but merely desired to refinance their homes were waiting even longer.

The buying spree had another pronounced effect on First Nationwide. A rise in operating expenses associated with First Nationwide's expansion, combined with lower interest margins, was hurting earnings. From a net income of $104 million in 1986, profits plummeted to $64 million in 1987 and to only $3.6 million in 1988. That was the year Ford decided to send in one of its own, John Devine, who came from its trucks division, where he had previously been controller. Devine instituted a cost-cutting program to reduce the number of employees by 10 percent—roughly 500 jobs—and reduced expenses by one fourth in two years.

Game . . .

While First Nationwide was cutting expenses and growing via an acquisition shopping list, something quite different was going on approximately 450 miles south in Pasadena, California. Angelo Mozilo and David Loeb, the founders and leaders of mortgage banker Countrywide Credit Industries, were also ambitiously enacting a plan for nationwide growth. This strategy was based on developing a unique, low-cost distribution system; developing state-of-the-art data-processing applications and communications networks; implementing innovative, efficient processes; and radically improving customer service, all of which came into focus at its front line field agents. That front line included mortgage officers who were salaried—rather than commissioned as was the case at First Nationwide and most other mortgage lenders in the United States—and who received bonuses on Countrywide's corporate performance.

One thing that Countrywide wasn't doing was buying other banks, nor was it cutting costs by optimizing operations. Rather than tinkering with an existing loan origination method, Countrywide devised a completely new approach to loan origination, based on advanced technology and infrastructure, frontline empowerment and enablement, and customer focus. While traditional mortgage lenders promised to complete an application approval process in 45 to 90 days, Countrywide Credit set out to make loan approval decisions in just hours and later in mere minutes! The typical loan approval process at an established institution in 1990 involved fourteen to sixteen different participants, followed by a trip to the loan committee. The loan committee at a typical mortgage lender met once a month, and unfortunate applicants missing a piece of the package could well find themselves waiting for the next meeting. Countrywide's novel process was designed around "a loan committee of one"—the frontline agent who processes the customer's loan application. Countrywide's agents benefited from highly sophisticated information systems that allowed access to third-party databases, such as consumer credit history information, and sophisticated scoring systems to measure loan quality. Agents were provided with decision support systems to help them make loan decisions on the spot, moving marginal applications into the green zone by adjusting loan-to-value ratios down to more favorable levels.

Not only did Countrywide's new process provide massive improvements in customer service, but it also reduced variable costs for a loan transaction to a small fraction of its traditional competitors' costs. By 1991, it was only $748 per loan versus an industry average of $2,357. Countrywide's game plan was to turn the cost, quality, and service edge provided by its state-of-the-art business practices into market leadership in the national mortgage business. Although Countrywide may not have been much more than a blip on First Nationwide's radar in 1989, things were about to change.

In 1989, Countrywide set up a division to market directly to consumers—a presage of industry changes to come. Previously it had marketed exclusively through intermediaries such as mortgage brokers. The company was experiencing increased loan demand and improved margins as the S and Ls' problems reduced pricing pressure. It had a broad, well-organized distribution system and had instituted a national toll-free telephone service.

Countrywide wasn't expanding by purchasing bankrupt S and Ls; rather, they expanded by opening $30,000-a-shot retail branches. By 1990, there were 100 of them in 24 states. It cost Countrywide in the neighborhood of $2.7 million to open those 100 offices. First Nationwide had 284 branches in fifteen states, but fourteen of those states had been entered in the 1980s by purchasing other S and Ls for hundreds of millions of dollars. Existing business came with those mostly troubled or insolvent S and Ls, but it was not always quality business. In contrast, because Countrywide was a pure mortgage banker and not a portfolio lender, it was free from the credit risks of lenders who kept loans on their own books, although because it resold its mortgage debt, it maintained con-

Figure 4.5
Countrywide Credit's "Break-Out"

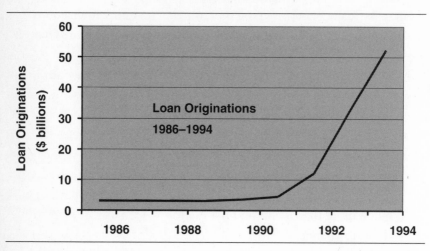

stant vigilance on issues of quality. Furthermore, Countrywide's average cost to originate a mortgage continued to drop. By 2000, it was only $223 per loan. Like virtually all process breakthroughs, Countrywide enjoyed much lower costs, dramatically superior service, shorter cycle times, and more, as its loan volumes soared (see Figure 4.5).

Meanwhile, in Northern California, Nationwide announced in 1989 that it would close the 170 small branches it had opened in Kmart discount stores because they had failed to attract enough deposits. In a statement, Chairman Robert Lackovic said:

> First Nationwide is developing a more focused strategy. We are concentrating more closely on the opportunities presented by our recent acquisitions, on meeting our customers' needs in the banks new and old markets, as well as on the company's profitability.

In 1990 and 1991, First Nationwide lost a total of $184 million, blamed on the thrift's mortgage securities portfolio and a poorly timed venture into commercial lending. In early 1991, Ford named Devine to First Nationwide's chief executive position and brought in a former Citicorp executive as President. Nonetheless, the company was well into the red, and later that year Ford had to pump in an unexpected infusion of $250 million to bolster its weakened financial condition. Problem loans by this point required more than $450 million in loan loss set-asides by Ford.

. . . Set,

By 1991, on the other hand, upstart Countrywide was the number eight loan originator in the "vital" Southern California market, and First Nationwide was hanging on to 25th place by its fingernails, with only one third of Countrywide's volume. The focus for First Nationwide Bank now, in defensive incumbent fashion, was on cutting costs and finding a way to cleanse its portfolio of bad branches and loans. "We . . . are encouraged by our continued focus on cost and quality," Devine said in mid-1991, announcing a plan to lay off another 10 percent of First Nationwide's workforce.[11]

By that time, some observers said, the money Ford had put into First Nationwide would have been enough to develop a new car line. The term *black hole* was being bandied about at Ford headquarters. First Nationwide began divesting many of the operations it had purchased in the late eighties, a total of nearly 70 branches in six states.

. . . Match!

In 1992, First Nationwide posted a $60 million loss. By 1993 it had shrunk to only 213 branches in nine states. CEO John Devine said at that time that the shrinkage was likely to continue: "Our long term strategy is to focus our distribution on fewer markets."

In 1992, Countrywide Credit, on the other hand, earned a profit of $123 million, up 173 percent from the prior year. It lent $32 billion, more than any bank or S and L in the United States. And thanks to the quality controls it used in selecting mortgages, defaults were actually going down.[12] Countrywide had moved into the position of market leader in mortgage originations. Riding the power of new technologies and new business processes, the insurgent had seized market leadership right out from under the noses of the established players. While revitalized incumbents Wells, Chase, and Bank of America were now regrouping to reenter the market with services comparable to the new standards, Countrywide was pursuing a second breakthrough. By the mid-1990s, Countrywide developed its Platinum Extranet designed to bring its infrastructure and business support systems to third-party mortgage originators. It brought the same efficiency, service, and quality levels to independent loan brokers as it had done with its own agents. Mortgage brokers, credit unions, S and Ls, and even banks used Countrywide's business systems to originate home loans, leveraging the company's own operations.

Countrywide was also aggressively and successfully utilizing artificial intelligence to process loan applications, and it was effectively integrating direct online channels with its low-cost retail office network. It was well-prepared to compete in the home loan market of the 2000s. While mammoth Ford could only lick its wounds and lumber away, and while First Nationwide/Cal Fed was now back to playing a regional game, insurgent Countrywide Credit had elbowed its way into the big time.

Glory Days

Countrywide's momentum has accelerated in the mortgage market boom of the past few years. Loan originations in 2002 totaled $252 billion, an 82 percent increase over the previous year's total and the fastest rate of growth among the top ten lenders (see Table 4.2). A staggering $102 billion in fundings were recorded in the fourth quarter alone. Net revenues, which had doubled from $1.6 billion in 1997 to $3.6 billion in 1999, continued to grow at an impressive pace. Total revenues for 2002 topped $7 billion.

Table 4.2
Top Home Mortgage Originators in 2002
Excluding Subprime. Dollars in Millions
Published April 15, 2003

Rank		Volume			Market Share	
		2002	2001	Change	2002	Change
1	Wells Fargo Home Mortgage	$329,221	$196,732	67.34%	12.08%	2.01%
2	Washington Mutual	$311,959	$175,537	77.72%	11.44%	2.46%
3	Countrywide Financial Corp	$251,901	$138,194	82.28%	9.24%	2.17%
4	Chase Home Finance	$155,680	$184,202	-15.42%	5.71%	-3.71%
5	ABN Amro Mortgage	$117,779	$81,684	44.19%	4.32%	0.14%
6	Bank of America	$88,050	$84,065	4.74%	3.23%	-1.07%
7	National City Mortgage	$79,478	$56,865	39.77%	2.92%	0.01%
8	GMAC Residential Holdings	$71,617	$51,821	38.20%	2.63%	-0.02%
9	Cendant Mortgage	$59,280	$44,522	33.15%	2.17%	-0.1%
10	Homecomings/CMAC-RFC	$52,591	$35,724	47.21%	1.93%	0.1%
	Top 10	$1,517,556	$1,049,354	44.62%	55.67%	1.97%
	Total	$2,370,244	$1,698,942	39.51%	86.96%	-0.21%

Source: National Mortgage News.

Net income rose accordingly from $257 million in 1997 to $410 million in 2001, and to $841 million in 2002. That amazing record of success is not the whole story. In 2002, Countrywide Credit changed its name to Countrywide Financial, reflecting its transformation into a provider of a broad range of financial services. Founder Angelo Mozilo put it this way in 2001: "Our Company is in the midst of a dramatic and far reaching transformation. Evidence of this strategic shift is everywhere."

While Countrywide's consumer home loan origination business was booming, new lines of business were growing even faster. Countrywide has expanded beyond mortgage lending into banking, capital markets, and insurance lines of business. Pretax earnings from these new financial services doubled in 2002 to $375 million, reaching 28 percent of total earnings in the first quarter of 2003. Countrywide's new lines of business leverage two of the company's core competencies—capital market operations and retail consumer services. On the capital market side, Countrywide provides wholesale credit lines to mortgage market institutions and actively buys and sells mortgage and other securities. On the retail side, it operates a fast-growing bank and has entered the property and casualty insurance business. Insurance policies in force grew by almost 1 million to 4.2 million units in 2002. It also has a stable mortgage loan servicing portfolio that now exceeds $500 billion. With these new lines of business, Countrywide has other horses to pull its wagon when the home lending boom subsides.

THE EMPIRE STRIKES BACK

Let's not assume that insurgents and breakout niche players are always best at the breakthrough game. Established incumbents can innovate as well. In a growing number of markets, agile incumbents dominate new-wave, next-generation business models. We need look no further than the extended financial service sector.

Insurgent Countrywide Credit became market leader in the home mortgage business in the early 1990s but relinquished its lead to rejuvenated incumbents Norwest, Bank of America, and Chase by 1995. It would come back to secure a position in the inner circle of the home lending industry. In online banking, the insurgents never even got on the scoreboard. Internet-only insurgent banks appeared to be poised to capture the online banking market from older, mortar-based companies. But quite the opposite has happened. As a group, net-based banks have managed to garner only a microscopic share of U.S. bank deposits.[13] Of the top ten online banks, all are arms of established institutions. The incumbent never even let the new guys on the playing field, sweeping the top ten spots in e-banking by 1999 (see Figure 4.6).

These agile incumbents stand out from the rest of the banking industry. By mid-2000, only 625 of the nation's 9,000 consumer banks offered online banking. A 1999 study by Forrester Research found that a mere 10 percent of U.S. account holders were banking online, and 2 percent of U.S. households were paying bills online. Yet, despite the limited development of the online banking market, a number of old-time banks were all over the emerging opportunity.

Insurgents were active in the market, some with significant promise. Among the earliest pure Internet banks were Security First Network Bank, Netbank, and CompuBank. These e-banks took advantage of lower costs compared to bricks-and-mortar banks to offer higher rates of return on deposits, money market accounts, and checking accounts. In addition to a host of insurgents, convergent companies climbing on the Web bankwagon included Intuit, which has evolved from a financial software firm into a full-service financial services company; Nordstrom's, which applied for a unitary thrift charter to become a bank[14]; and E★Trade, which purchased Telebank and renamed it E★Trade Bank. E★Trade also bought a network of 8,000 automated teller machines (ATMs) to establish a ground presence that could be linked with both bank and brokerage accounts.[15]

Figure 4.6
1999 e-Banking Market Share

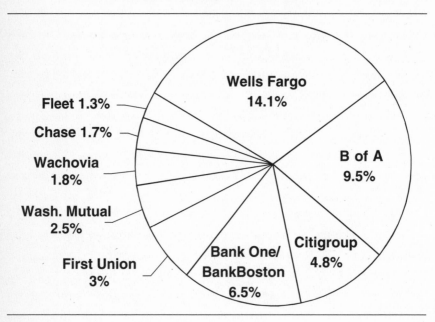

Source: Gomez Advisors Inc.

Convergent competitors from the extended financial service sector were also introducing online-banking services. In mid-2000, Merrill Lynch announced that it would team with Hong Kong and Shanghai Banking Corporation (HSBC). Holdings to offer online banking and investment services throughout Europe and Asia. In 2000, GE Financial Network added e-banking service to the array of financial services offered on its Web site. Its e-bank offerings were developed in conjunction with CompuBank, in which GE has invested.

The reaction of the more forward-looking large banks, however, has demonstrated the ability of large organizations with bricks-and-mortar presence to blunt the charge of the e-bank insurgents and convergents while building a new channel for themselves. Wells Fargo was one of the first large banks to move onto the Internet. Rather than creating a separate business unit to pursue online banking, Wells Fargo allowed its business lines to pursue Internet ventures directly.[16] By 1998, it had some 620,000 home banking customers, compared to 500,000 for Nations-Bank, 250,000 for Chase, and 200,000 for Bank of America.[17] By early 2000, Bank of America, Wells Fargo, and First Union each claimed to have more than 1 million customers for their online services.[18]

Chase, despite its rank among the giant banks, has lagged its peers in exploiting the Internet. Chase.com was formed as a separate unit in an attempt to let it develop outside the bank's bureaucracy.[19] Will Chase be able to join the online banking leaders while simultaneously digesting J.P. Morgan? They can only hope that online banking develops slowly, giving them a chance to catch up. Meanwhile, Wells Fargo's more agile and integrated online initiatives have been rewarded with a substantial value share premium over its New York rival, as seen in Figure 4.7.

Citigroup, another New York-based giant, has long been a progressive, innovative participant in the financial services sector. Yet it also has had its difficulties developing an online presence, largely it seems because it also insisted on spinning out its internet play. Created by the merger of Citibank and Travelers, Citigroup is the largest and most profitable financial institution in the world with total assets of $717 billion and pretax profits in 1999 of $15.9 billion. It has become the inner-circle champion in the financial services supersector.

Like Chase, Citibank created a separate business unit for its Internet effort.[20] John Reed, then cochairman and co-chief executive of Citigroup with Sandy Weill of Travelers, took personal charge of the Internet operation in July 1999. Reed wanted to develop a self-contained online retail financial-services provider and spent over $500 million on the effort. Called e-Citi, it attracted few customers and reportedly was resented by other Citigroup businesses. It was downgraded to an incubator

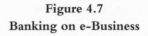

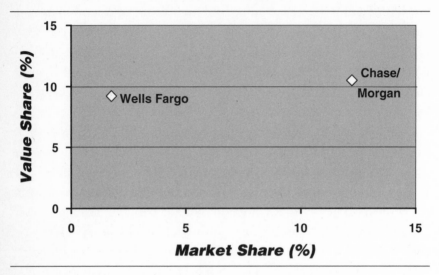

Figure 4.7
Banking on e-Business

Sources: Federal Reserve System National Information Center, FDIC.

after Reed retired.[21] Citibank also started up a stand-alone Internet bank called Citi f/i. By mid-2000, however, after it had only been in operation for a year, Citibank announced that the Web bank would be integrated with its online service. Even with these missteps, Citibank lurked just behind the leaders in online banking.

Despite its stumbles, Citibank has consistently set its controls for the heart of the emerging financial services inner circle and has consistently been an early participant in emerging technologies, services, and markets. It may yet find the model for grafting online banking into its core business, thereby solidifying its new status as market champion in financial services.

Established market leaders can make the leap to next-generation business models, reshaping themselves and their markets in the process. In the next sections, we look at the unique position of the market leader in more depth. First, let's look in the dregs of a highly competitive market to prove that any company can aspire to and achieve breakthrough.

Old Dogs . . .

Here's a quick look at how a disrespected senior citizen found new life. By the late 1990s, Mervyn's had been the sad sack in the Dayton–Hudson (now Target) family for some years. Overshadowed by its larger sibling, Target, Mervyn's got no respect. By the late 1990s there were frequent and public discussions about selling or closing the business. Kohl's, a new and improved, next-generation version of the Mervyn's concept, was expanding rapidly, further threatening a weakened franchise. Mervyns' new CEO Bart Butzer and his team took that talk seriously and decided to take their fate into their own hands. At a session I led in January 1999, the team embraced a single outrageous objective and decided to live or die in its pursuit.

Mervyns' breakthrough program focused on two interconnected goals: significantly increasing stock availability on the store shelves while radically reducing total inventory. The day after the senior team embraced this outrageous objective, Mervyns' director of merchandise planning abruptly quit, claiming that these goals were impossible. Undaunted, the Mervyn's team, led by chief financial officer (CFO) Chuck Lynch, took up the challenge and devised a breakthrough program to significantly increase Mervyns' stock availability with reduced inventory holdings. Mervyns' new purchasing and stocking strategy required breaking one of retailing's sacred cows, the "open-to-buy" procurement system. In brief, Mervyn's imposed a set of disciplines on purchasing and merchandising managers to tailor these activities according to key Stock Keeping Unit (SKU) and store characteristics. The impact of these operating innovations kicked in quickly.

Within one year, Mervyn's achieved dramatic improvements in stock availability, with an in-stock ratio in the 98 percent range and significant reductions in total inventory. Another key result of this program was a reduction in markdown activity of some $150 million. Most important was that Mervyns' return on sales rose sharply from 5.0 percent in 1999 to 7.1 percent in 2001. Mervyns' pretax profit increased a whopping 31 percent in 2000. In that year, Mervyns' management team received higher total bonus compensation than their big brothers at Target. Within another year, Mervyns' CEO was promoted to head Target, bringing key members of his team—and the Mervyn's breakthrough program—along with him. Mervyn's had moved from being the sick sister in the Dayton-Hudson retail group to become the family hero.

Mervyns' breakthrough program may not be enough to change its market position, but it was able to trigger and enjoy a new success cycle. Perhaps more important was that it supplied a senior leadership team and a breakthrough program to benefit Target in its ongoing competition with market champion Wal-Mart. Added to Target's renowned merchandising and guest experience competencies, its in-stock initiative makes the Minneapolis retailer an even more formidable competitor. But its biggest asset may be breakthrough thinking. In 2002, Target embraced a new breakthrough strategy. Its new objective is beyond outrageous. It aims to become "the best company in the world," and it is shaping a focused enterprise strategy to achieve that audacious goal.

Mervyns' experience shows that even the most downtrodden market participant can embrace and achieve outrageous objectives. Furthermore, Mervyns' management team, who may have had little to lose, won the opportunity to drive the Target Stores race car in the big race, all because they had the courage to embrace an outrageous objective and execute a breakthrough strategy. That task may have been easier because their back was to the wall and they had no other real options, but that does not diminish their accomplishment. In their case, a breakthrough strategy was necessary to survive and start a new success cycle. Not all firms in such situations are able to make that leap.

NOTES

1. "Solid Worldwide 3Q 2000 PC Demand with 18.5% Unit Growth," IDC news release on second quarter 2000 PC sales, Sept. 7, 2000. Company news release:"Dell Takes No. 1 Spot in Worldwide Workstation Shipments," Aug. 21, 2000. "Y2K Didn't Slow PC Server Sales in 1999, IDC Reveals," International Data Corporation news release, Feb. 2, 2000. "Explosive Small Business PC and Server Purchases Via the Internet Channel Propel Direct Vendor Gains," Access Markets International news release, Sept. 11, 2000.

2. For a discussion of these generic breakthrough strategies, see S. Davis and W. Davidson, *2020 Vision,* Simon and Schuster (New York), 1992.

3. Leah Nathans Spiro, "Merrill's E-Battle," BusinessWeek Online, Nov. 15, 1999, cover story.

4. "Discount Brokerage Firms Agree to Merge," *New York Times,* June 18, 1981, p. D-4.

5. "US Banks Invade Brokerage Business but "Bull" Sees No Red Flag, So Far," *Christian Science Monitor,* July 26, 1982, p. 10.

6. "The Changes in Discounting," *New York Times,* July 10, 1981, p. D-8.

7. From company PR materials.

8. Schwab news release, PR Newswire, Jan. 19, 1999.

9. David Wanetick, "Online Brokerage Frenzy Threatens Banks," *Web Finance,* June 7, 1999, p. 9.

10. "Online Brokerage Storms Back after Poor Third Quarter," US Bancorp Piper Jaffray news release, Feb. 2, 2000.

11. Jeff Pelline, "Red Ink Flows at SF's First Nationwide," *San Francisco Chronicle,* July 26, 1991, p. C1.

12. Michael Flagg, "Pasadena Lender Thrives in Sluggish Housing Market," *Los Angeles Times,* April 27, 1993, p. D2-33.

13. Edmund Sanders, "To Assure Customers They're Real, Virtual Banks Are Getting Physical," *Los Angeles Times,* Aug. 6, 2000, p. C1.

14. William Streeter, "E-commerce Killer," ABA Banking Online, January 2000, www.ababj.com.

15. Patrick McGeehan, "Banks Are Slow to Move Online, But So Are Their Customers," *New York Times,* June 7, 2000, p. H6.

16. Kenneth Cline, "Mobilizing for E-Strategy," *Banking Strategies,* March/April 2000.

17. Jason K. Krause, "Wells Fargo and the Wild, Wild Web," TheStandard.com, Feb. 17, 2000.

18. "Online Banking is Exceeding Forecast," *Cincinnati Post,* Nov. 29, 1999.

19. Kenneth Cline, "Mobilizing for E-Strategy," *Banking Strategies,* March/April 2000.

20. Kenneth Cline, "Mobilizing for E-Strategy," *Banking Strategies,* March/April 2000.

21. "First Among Equals," *The Economist,* U.S. edition, Aug. 26, 2000.

CHAPTER 5

THE MINDSET OF THE MARKET LEADER

LET'S LOOK briefly at two more breakthrough retailers, now at different stages in their success cycle. In the mid-1990s, a new company entered the U.S. "remote retail" business. Although it was not the first mover in exploiting the new channel, the firm had a compelling vision: Begin with a single merchandise line, grab sales from mortar-based competitors by discounting at levels they can't match, and offer ease of ordering and reliable delivery. As people chat about the new firm, sales begin to skyrocket—not by percents, but by multiples. With no storefronts to worry about, the company concentrated on ramping up its strategically located warehouse operations to handle the unprecedented number of orders. It began to expand its offerings into a broad range of general merchandise, moving into the mainstream of retailing. As the insurgent grabbed market share, brick-based competitors—those not in denial at the dawn of a new century—realized that things would never be the same again. Can you name the company?

It was Sears Roebuck. And the "new century" was the twentieth. But

Figure 5.1
A Century Apart

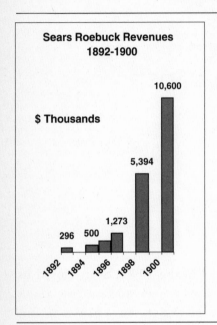

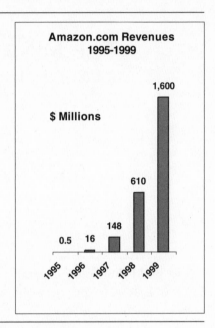

Sources: *"1890s America: A Chronology"* and annual reports.

the growth parallels with today's mass merchandising insurgent, Amazon.com, are striking, as seen in Figure 5.1. Richard W. Sears began his business by selling watches in the late 1800s, and his company later went on to offer a huge selection of goods in its famous catalogues, surpassing competitor Montgomery Ward in 1900 and going on to dominate its industry. Indeed, Sears was the first retail operation named to the Dow Jones industrial average.[1]

Amazon.com started out small as well, selling mail-order books on the World Wide Web in the late 1900s and then growing quickly. Although it captured only 5.4 percent of the $24-billion U.S. book market during 1999,[2] Amazon dominated the burgeoning Internet channel, with 80 percent of online book sales.[3] Maintaining its leadership, it has since expanded into a growing line of merchandise. While continuing to grow at a healthy pace, Amazon is now profitable. Sales grew by 25 percent in 2002 to just under $4 billion, and Amazon pared its net loss from $550 million in 2001 to $150 million in 2002. In 2003, 60 percent below its market high, Amazon was still worth $14.8 billion, dwarfing Barnes and Noble ($1.1 billion), Borders ($1.1 billion), and BarnesandNoble.com ($50 million). Indeed, Amazon was twice as valuable as Sears ($6.8 billion)—perhaps a more appropriate comparison, given the growing breadth and success of the product offerings in its online catalog.

Sears meanwhile had long since slipped into the meat locker of the retail sector, its ignominy compounded by its removal from the Dow Jones average. Ironically, Sears could have been an early Internet leader. It once held 50 percent of Prodigy, one of the first commercialized online services, but sold its stake in 1996. While e-tailers were rushing to build their remote retail model in the 1990s, Sears closed its catalog operations in 1993 and sold its 30 percent stake in high-speed data networking company Advantis to IBM in 1997 for $450 million. Two years later, IBM sold its global Internet communications network, of which Advantis was a major component, to AT&T for $5 billion. Like so many incumbents, Sears missed the emerging business market, not so much for lack of insight, investment, or effort, but because it blinked.

In terms of its retail operations, although it continues to lead in sales of appliances, Sears has stolidly remained a middle-of-the-road general merchandise retail chain store operation, mining a stagnant vein of the retail market that has hovered around $40 billion in recent years, even as the sales volume of discount stores has rocketed to almost $400 billion.[4] As late as the 1980s Sears was still the dominant retailer in the United States, but it lost touch with its customers, who migrated to specialty stores, category killers, and discount retailers. Closing unprofitable stores, reorganizing, pitching the store's purported fashion sense to streetwise consumers and other tweaks have not provided the turnaround Sears seeks. The long-time market champion seems destined to play a fading role for the foreseeable future. Sears has been on a long, sustained decline for decades, its position of market leadership lost long ago. The twentieth century marked a full cycle for this American institution, from insurgent to premium growth company to market champion to decline and marginalization. Yet, Sears' steady spiral shows just how hard it is to kill a market leader. Champions can create market franchises with long half-lives, and these firms may endure long after they have been displaced from center stage. Still, Sears has lost its grip on the retail sector, and the mantle of market leadership has passed to a new generation. Sears' fate would seem to await all established market leaders.

THE INCUMBENT'S DILEMMA

A successful incumbent becomes so by dint of hard and heroic effort, hard-won insights, and hard-fought campaigns to perfect and protect a profitable business model. It takes great effort and investment to build a winning enterprise—and even more to change it! Many incumbents find themselves unable to master the forces of change in their markets. Some appear frozen in the face of clear impending transitions. What are the principal sources of paralysis? Try this list for starters.

Legacy Factors

The winning formula that propelled incumbents to market leadership manifests itself in many forms. Existing processes and practices become deeply embedded and take on a life of their own, limiting a firm's ability to adapt to more effective models. The mortgage lending industry establishment failed to see and seize opportunities to streamline their existing processes and ceded leadership to innovators Countrywide Credit and others. Much of the book publishing industry today still uses traditional production processes, resulting in 12-month lead times to convert manuscripts into finished books, even though new processes could readily cut lead times by 90 percent.

Information systems (ISs) universally present a substantial legacy anchor. Antiquated information systems, many more than 20 years old, greatly inhibit established firms' ability to introduce new offerings or practices. Some established firms need the equivalent of IS archeologists to locate source code and to understand the civilization that created it. Mike Armstrong, as CEO of AT&T, commented that he had enjoyed selling computers to AT&T as a young IBM salesman but was surprised to see that those same machines were still there 25 years later.

AT&T is not alone. When a new product idea is being discussed inside an established telecom carrier, the bottleneck question is, "Can we bill it?" It can take six months or longer to enable billing for a simple product introduction, and complex products may prove impossible to bill. AT&T's attempt to implement an integrated offering of communication services, including wireless, cable, Internet access, and local and long distance in one package, was severely hampered by its inability to adapt its diverse operating systems to support unified provisioning and billing of the new package. Other established carriers face similar internal obstacles.

All obstacles are not internal. Existing channels of distribution can create formidable resistance to innovation. The CEO of a major life insurance firm told me the following not long ago:

> We will never circumvent our established agent channel. Over the past century we have built up the strongest network of dedicated life insurance sales agents in the industry, and we won't do anything to jeopardize that channel.

The most formidable obstacle to innovation, however, may be legacy culture and consciousness. The perspectives, concepts, and assumptions that prevail inside a company's collective consciousness and—perhaps even more important—those embedded in its subconscious lead the firm to deny or discount emerging realities. Think of Digital Equipment's (DEC) studied dismissal of the personal computer as a classic example of incumbent denial. To successfully innovate, an industry incumbent must—in a determined and wholesale way—abandon its commitment to legacy channels, processes, practices, products, technologies, business models, and mindsets. Without this high-anxiety action, the organization's focus will remain on incremental adaptation, and it will remain vulnerable to innovation.

Fear of Cannibalization

Often the future emerges from beneath the feet of market leaders—that is, in offerings that emerge at the low end of the marketplace, with lower unit prices and margins than the norm's. It may be for this reason that IBM was slow to enter the minicomputer market; DEC, in turn, denied the emerging microcomputer market; Xerox ceded the low end of the photocopier market to Japanese rivals; and Detroit's big three automakers have never excelled in the small-car segment. It's a classic dilemma for an established incumbent. Aggressive activity in an emerging low-end market can undo decades of effort aimed at creating a profitable market model. Although that economic dilemma is real enough, it is often misleading. Rarely do market transitions involve a one-to-one displacement of high-margin sales by low-margin units. More important, failure to capture an emerging market may concede substantial growth opportunities and even market leadership to insurgents. In the face of a low-end uprising, the incumbent is faced with a fundamental choice. Should it fight a rear-guard action to prolong its doomed market model and profit generator as long as possible while ceding share and leadership to insurgents? Or should it convert the established market to the new order of things itself? Few incumbents are willing to aggressively embrace the latter strategy.

Short–Run Financial Results

Many incumbent firms dedicate the bulk of their energy and attention to generating short-term financial results out of their current business model. They see themselves (often correctly) as walking a delicate tightrope where any financial shortfall will result in dire stock market penalties, which would leave the firm even more vulnerable. Yet undue focus on short-term results is the same as being penny-wise and pound-foolish. Incumbents frequently allow obsession with short-term financial results to overrule larger strategic priorities.

Inability to Leave the Comfort Zone

It is clear that many firms and executives simply do not want to leave those areas in which they are comfortable. Figure 5.2 shows a simple view

Figure 5.2
Change, Comfort, and Contribution

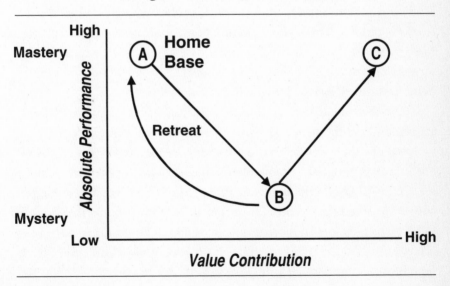

of this phenomenon. The goal is to move from mastery of the old world to mastery of the new.

It is difficult for anyone to migrate from perfected practices to new, mysterious activities and models in which they are initially unskilled and uncomfortable. This transition from old areas of excellence to new emerging competencies is the central challenge for the typical incumbent. Many individuals and firms will make visible efforts to embrace or adopt new practices but will retreat to established ways at the first opportunity. New activities involve substantial anxiety, discomfort, and uncertainty, and many will race back to the old ways, proclaiming, "I told you it wouldn't work." Only substantial coaching and counseling or massive replenishment of the organization can make this change effective. The essential challenge for all incumbents today is to abandon their comfort zone and move boldly into uncomfortable territory.

Lame-Duck Leadership

Transformation requires focused, relentless, and aggressive leadership. Many incumbent organizations promote leaders who are designed to be stewards and wardens of the established organization, not radical change masters. Stewardship is a virtue, but static stewardship can be fatal. A true steward aims not to leave the organization as he or she found it, but rather better positioned to face present and future realities.

Incumbent organizations also often have older leaders with relatively short tenures at the helm. Many of these leaders may not have the time window or other personal characteristics necessary to drive a successful breakthrough program. I remember a meeting with a potential client in which the CEO described how he intended to transform his established company. When I asked him for details, he told me I would have to talk to his colleague, Joe, about that. Joe, it seems, had been called out of retirement to lead the transformation effort for a year or two, after which time he could retire once again. We passed on that consulting opportunity. In an era that is increasingly unforgiving to incumbents, no single factor is a better predictor of success or failure than the quality of a company's senior leadership.

Distraction, Diversion, and Diversity

Even organizations with effective leaders and strong strategies for transformation will face this 3D problem. The most common source of distraction is the day-to-day demands of the business. It will always be easier to work on today's problem rather than on tomorrow's opportunity. Day-to-day operations and short-term financial results become a comfort zone of their own. One of the breakthrough firms we worked with had developed a master plan for creating a next-generation relational database, the world's largest, that would enable a series of new customer offerings and revenue streams. The new initiative involved a complete redesign of the company's core asset, a massive customer database. At one point, I asked the new initiative's director how everything was progressing. She replied, "We are now substantially behind schedule and the new platform will be introduced at least six months after our target date." I questioned her about the source of the delay. "I've lost 30 of my best programmers who have been pulled off to work on upgrades to the systems that we are supposed to replace," she said. Short-term emergencies, especially those that seem to be central to near-term financial results or customer requirements, can effectively dismantle long-term strategic initiatives.

Myopia

Ted Levitt's timeless tale about market myopia remains truer today than ever.[5] But today's railroads are truckers who think that their products are freight miles, telecom carriers who think they're in the voice telephony business, cable providers who think they're in the TV industry, retailers who think it's all about in-store shopping, and so on. Expansive thinking about markets can be central to value creation.

Myopia tends to be reinforced by peer pressure within industry groups. If one's competitive perspective is dominated by traditional rivals, myopia may be inevitable. Competitive strategy tends to converge within industry structures, and competition often becomes based on incremental improvements in cost and quality. Caught up in the game, such companies fail to look across the defined boundaries of competition at substitute product groups, adjacent industries, and other areas where fertile fields for innovation lie.[6]

The Fear Factor

Bet-the-company kind of change ought to frighten successful firms. Traditionally, only the most desperate companies have attempted it. Indeed, until recently, it would have represented the most abject failure of existing management. Fundamental innovation is the toughest, most frightening kind of change effort of all for a successful company that has devoted years of effort and tons of money to avoid the need for such desperate measures.

Radical innovation renders obsolete the very practices that built a company's current success. It wrecks carefully crafted product/service designs and painstakingly constructed business models. It causes hard-won incremental improvements to become suddenly irrelevant. It cannibalizes profitable business. It marginalizes what were once essential jobs. It obsoletes capital investments. For many firms, it takes a true crisis to force them to embrace breakthrough strategies.

All these factors and more inhibit innovation within incumbent market leaders. It has become mainstream management thought to assume that incumbents cannot be innovative and that they are sitting targets for disruptive competitors like those described in this book. Indeed, the typical incumbent market leader is likely to experience rigidity around its business model. Only those market leaders who win the battle for control of the innovations that will reshape their industries become market champions, and such companies exhibit a far different mindset from that of the archetype incumbent.

Staying Power

Everything changes so fast in this industry that even within a year, different kinds of leadership are needed from the CEO.

—Roger W. Johnson, Western Digital CEO, 1993

Enduring leaders deserve special recognition. What global industry today exhibits the same market leaders as it had in 1990? Few major industries can make that claim. Then this should shock you: One such industry is the disk drive industry—a sector that has introduced a new generation of technology every 11 months for the last decade-plus. It is a volatile, hypercompetitive, gunslinger technology business with a stable set of competitors. These incumbents have learned to play on the freeway.

Short technology cycles in the hard disk drive industry make it fertile ground for insurgents, but it would be a mistake to confuse technological instability during the last two decades with industry instability. The core competitors in this industry have been remarkably stable, experiencing minimal change in make-up or market position over the '90s decade, as seen in Figure 5.3

As a technological accomplishment, hard disk drives stand shoulder to shoulder with central processor chips—with the added complication that they are electromechanical devices. Yet the hard disk drive industry has easily surpassed Moore's law in price performance gains, as prices per megabyte plummet (see Figure 5.4). Data storage has been the most powerful of the key engines underlying the information economy.

The hard disk drive has met market needs for storage capacity, density

Figure 5.3
Market Share: Hard Disk Drives (1991–1999)

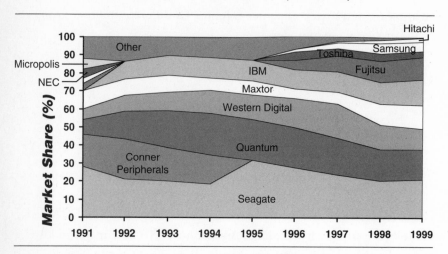

Sources: Dataquest, TrendFOCUS, California Technology Stock Letter.

requirements, and access speeds far in excess of what was envisioned only a decade ago. Despite the advent of data storage substitutes like flash memory, zip drives, and optical storage, hard disk drive (HDD) technology remains the main platform for PC data storage.[7]

Well over 200 companies have entered the HDD race during the past three decades. Many have failed, either exiting the business or perishing, including some with significant market shares. In 1990, 56 companies worldwide produced hard disk drives. A decade later, only 11 producers remained, and the top four commanded roughly 80 percent of the market.[8] After the industry free-for-all, these companies emerged as an inner circle of finely managed survivors. The survivors have now struggled so far down the essential technology and management curves underpinning this business that they seem fully capable of dominating the game even in the face of new threats.

Year after year, cycle after cycle, they have survived in the face of razor-thin margins in core market segments. They reorganize as necessary in

Figure 5.4
Price per Megabyte
Hard Disk Drives

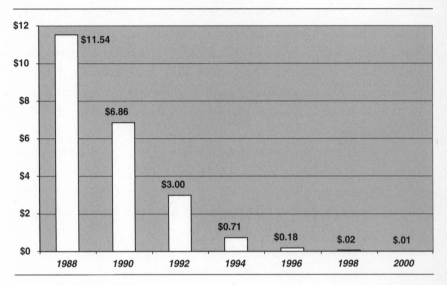

Source: DISK/TREND.

response to the demands of an $18 billion OEM market for smaller, faster, better, cheaper, more diverse requirements in design and manufacturing performance. The ability of these survivors to perennially reinvent themselves has ensured their continued domination of the business through successive generations of data storage technology. They are the fittest survivors and role models for incumbents who would endure.

PROFILE OF A MARKET CHAMPION

The HDD business exhibits a classic portrait of a market champion. Seagate Technology held a 21 percent market share as 2000 began, but was awarded over 70 percent of the industry's market cap. Over the past decade, the company had retained its market share while steadily increasing its value share. Seagate offers lessons for any market leader.

The eight-inch drive was already on the market when Seagate was founded in 1979. Involved with the disk storage business since its beginnings in 1955, cofounder Alan Shugart started Seagate with marketing whizzes Finis Connor, Thomas Mitchell, and Douglas Mahon, after Connor convinced Shugart that smaller 5.25-inch drives would sell well in the emerging personal computer market. With $30,000 in cash and $2 million in second mortgages on their houses, they set up shop in Scotts Valley, California.

In 1980, incumbent Control Data Corporation accounted for more than half the worldwide market for OEM HDDs, but Seagate quickly grabbed the market for the smaller drives. It was first to market with the 5.25-inch HDD, shipping 1,300 drives in its first year of production. This shoebox-sized device replaced the use of unreliable magnetic tape memories on desktop computers. Instead of using tape or tapping into a central computer, users could store large word processing, graphics, and spreadsheet applications on their desktop computers. Desktop data storage was truly a disruptive technology, which led to the distributed computing environment and the PC industry as we know it today.

Seagate thought big from the beginning. The eight-inch drive had been hampered when its makers failed to agree on standards and failed to ramp up production quickly enough. Conner avoided both issues by licensing Seagate's design to other companies, including Texas Instruments—thus creating the industry standard for 5.25-inch drives.[9] Among Seagate's first customers were Apple Computer and IBM's PC division. When a banker warned Finis Conner in 1982 that Seagate was moving too quickly and might run aground, Conner replied: "Run aground! If that's going to happen, I want to be moving so fast that we'll run 400 yards up on the beach." No one could better state what it takes to seize leadership in an emerging market.

From $10 million in 1980, Seagate's revenues soared to $344 million and earnings hit $37 million in 1984, based in part on a huge OEM contract with IBM. The firm raised $72 million in a 1982 stock offering and used the money to quintuple U.S. production, open an R&D center, and build a plant in Singapore to produce subassemblies. Seagate was already the acknowledged champion of the disk drive market, with a consistent share of over 40 percent. It dominated the low end, which included PCs and the segment for add-on drives. Already, Seagate had developed low-cost foreign suppliers for every component except the disk itself.

Seagate's next major move was to implement a vertical integration strategy to lock up its position as lowest cost producer. It started making disk drive heads in its Asian facilities. A pack of new competitors had entered the market, attracted by low entry costs ($5 million to organize and build a prototype; $15 million to achieve production), the availability of parts to construct drives, and a looming market of considerable size. Seagate, however, was well along on the learning curve and already had more than 200 OEM customers, now including DEC, HP, Honeywell, and AT&T. Even so, it was dependent on IBM for up to 50 percent of its revenues.

Seagate's first major blunder occurred in 1984. It was finishing a record fiscal year in which it shipped 757,000 ten-megabyte disk drives—nearly two thirds of them to IBM. The company announced new half-height, higher capacity 5.25-inch drives. But due to production and quality problems, Seagate couldn't supply the products and had to withdraw them from the market. Faced with this failure, company leaders decided to stick with tried-and-true technologies for the time being. "We don't need to be first in the market with leading-edge technology, we just need to be the leading volume supplier," Conner said.[10] Therein lay the seeds of the serious problems that Seagate would soon face.

Glory days don't last long in the disk drive industry. Floppy drive maker Tandon Corporation began a price war, seeking a foothold in the low end by undercutting Seagate's mass-market 10-megabyte drive. Then the bomb dropped: IBM, the largest OEM purchaser, took a large portion of its drive production in-house. One supplier went bankrupt; another lost 80 percent of its business. IBM constituted 60 percent of Seagate's business in 1984; the canceled orders cut Seagate's revenues in half. IBM also began equipping its PCs with new, 20-megabyte drives from another company, Computer Memories. In days, the wholesale price of 10-megabyte drives plunged from $430 to $320. Seagate responded quickly: Executives gathered around a table and disassembled a disk drive, calculating how much less each component would have to cost in order for the company to remain profitable at the lower price. Parts vendors across the United States and Asia were told not to ship unless they could meet the new, lower prices. Seagate's California manufacturing plants were relocated to Singapore, and 900 employees were laid off. Revenues plunged by half—yet the company still managed to eke out a profit while it struggled to catch up to the moving target of industry price-performance leadership.[11]

Things got worse in 1988. Seagate expanded its capacity to produce 5.25-inch drives just as that segment was eclipsed by sales of new, 3.5-inch hard drives. A rapidly growing market for laptop computers was stimulating demand for the new drives, and the latest IBM and Apple desktops incorporated the new 3.5-inch drives—but Seagate's production was still 90 percent 5.25-inch drives. In March 1988, Seagate lost 50 percent of its contract with Apple Computer. Seagate stock, which a year earlier had reached $34.25, plunged from $18.50 to $10.25 in four days after an August announcement that the firm would show a quarterly loss. The company was forced to cut production and lay off 200 U.S. employees. However, ongoing price wars—initiated by Seagate—hurt most other participants in the industry even more. Cash reserves dried up, losses reached record levels, and a half-dozen large manufacturers went bankrupt.

Seagate was beginning to operate like an ossified incumbent, missing out on emerging technologies and ceding next-generation opportunities to insurgent competitors. Finis Conner, who had left Seagate to found Conner Peripherals, noted in 1988, "Seagate has missed the transition from 16 to 32 bit drives. They don't have the products to bridge that gap."[12]

Seagate began to lose valuable share to Quantum, Connor Peripherals, and other competitors.

1989 saw incursions into the OEM market by IBM, Sony, and HP as well as preparations by other large hardware firms to enter the market. Corporate size and market share were becoming increasingly important to survival. Seagate addressed the size issue by acquiring Imprimis Technology, General Data's maker of high-performance hard drives. Whereas Seagate had been a chronically late entrant but a hard-nosed seller that won share with lowball prices, Imprimis brought it new manufacturing methods and a higher level of engineering, superior R&D talent, and much-needed quality control capabilities. The buy also gave Seagate a broader product line and new distribution channels to OEM customers. As the 1980s ended, Seagate was the only vendor that produced its own components, and it had the broadest product line of all: from low-end 3.5-inch drives for PCs to high-capacity 5.25- and 8-inch drives for servers, minicomputers, and mainframes. Seagate also continued to compete aggressively on price, and ongoing price wars forced a number or marginal competitors to abandon market segments or drop out of the business altogether.

Seagate's moves were trumped when Conner Peripherals announced revenue of $704.9 million for fiscal 1989, its third full year of operation; that marked Conner as the fastest-growing manufacturing start-up in history. And although Seagate was still master of the 5.25-inch drive market, Conner took advantage of Seagate's tardiness in smaller drives to capture roughly 90 percent of the 3.5-inch drive market for laptop computers. Moreover, Conner had about 57 percent of the burgeoning 2.25-inch drive market, and Conner would go on to capture the lead in 1.8-inch drives for notebook computers. Connor would seize overall market share leadership in 1992, yet Seagate would dominate the 1990s even more than it had the 1980s.

The Making of a Market Champion

As the 1990s began, Seagate had shipped 25 million disk drives and had become a multibillion dollar multinational with well over 30,000 employees. Customers could choose from nearly 200 disk-drive models with capacities ranging from 20 megabytes to 2.5 gigabytes and average access times as low as 10 milliseconds. But Seagate had barely time to digest Imprimis when a huge buildup of outmoded inventory again drove manufacturers' losses to record levels. In the 1991 price war, 16 disk drive manufacturers left the market.

Seagate learned from the 1991 price war that companies with quality problems suffered doubly in industry downturns. Disk drive makers by then had also learned that they had to save as much cash as possible during profitable times in order to have the $30 million to $40 million it would cost them to develop the next-generation drive platform, often in the face of a loss-creating price war. Seagate finished this market cycle bloodied but still standing as market champion (see Figure 5.5).

After a year of recovery in 1992, the most intense price wars yet began in 1993 after Conner and Maxtor were late to ship 175-megabyte drives. They tried to recoup the lost business by cutting prices on older drives that were still in demand. The resultant price wars meant losses for five of the six major HDD makers. Average drive prices declined about 50 percent, more than twice the normal rate. Indeed, prices dropped so far that although unit shipments were up sharply for 1993, industry revenue declined by a billion dollars from $19 billion to $18 billion.[13] No longer relying primarily on the hypercompetitive, low-end PC market, Seagate remained in the black throughout the downturn. It did lose market share, however, and Quantum became the leading drive supplier in 1993 with a 20.7 percent market share. Nevertheless, Quantum paid a price, losing $445 million on revenues of $2.2 billion. Following Quantum were Seagate with 19.9 percent, Conner with 18.7 percent and Western Digital

Figure 5.5
Hard Drive Makers: 1992

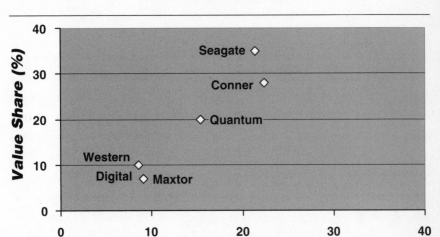

with 10 percent. Maxtor had been weakened by the price war and required a cash infusion from Hyundai.

Conner Peripherals' brief reign as market share leader was over. "The industry has undergone fundamental structural changes in the last 18 months," was the opinion of Finis Conner. "There has been a transition to commodity products with limited technical differentiation and severe price pressure, where price alone is the key competitive point."[14]

Alan Shugart had different perceptions, however. He was determined to use Seagate's newfound technical muscle, along with its massive manufacturing capability, to enter as many new segments as possible as early as possible. Shugart increased research and development efforts with a goal of setting industry standards for performance, reliability, and price. Besides the core skill set of making disk drives, he wanted Seagate to develop storage devices and software for handling text, graphics, audio, and video. The target was to double sales from $3 billion in 1993 to $6 billion by 2000, of which $1 billion would be from memory management software. Seagate's full-line strategy was clearly paying dividends, as its profitability stayed well above its peers'.

By 1993, Seagate ranked among the 200 largest industrial corporations in the United States, with $3 billion in revenue, more than 40,000 employees, and operations in 17 countries. It had just introduced a new range of hard drives that placed it at the front of the pack. It made its first buy of a software firm, a database company named Caltex. It continued to invest heavily in upgrading existing production facilities or building new ones, a practice it has maintained almost every year since its initial investment in Singapore in 1982. Seagate's vertical integration was also paying off as its components unit ensured availability of critical parts when competitors experienced shortages from suppliers. Seagate's profitability remained strong, yet Shugart had not been able to sell Seagate back into the industry lead, and Quantum retained overall market share leadership in 1994 (see Figure 5.6).

Consolidating the Leadership Position

Seagate's Shugart solved his market share problem in 1995 by acquiring prodigal son Conner Peripherals for $1.1 billion. The purchase, the largest of six Seagate made that year, created a company with annual revenues of nearly $8 billion, vaulting Seagate past Quantum and giving it command over one third of the HDD market. The move strengthened Seagate's position in the desktop and mobile PC markets, complementing its dominance in the high-capacity market. It also gave Seagate Conner's software and tape drive business, adding to its growing portfolio of data management and software operations and placing Shugart within shooting distance of his stated $1 billion goal for software sales. From being exclusively a supplier of 5.25-inch drives, 65,000-employee Seagate had transformed itself into the most complete company in the industry. Its

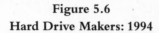

Figure 5.6
Hard Drive Makers: 1994

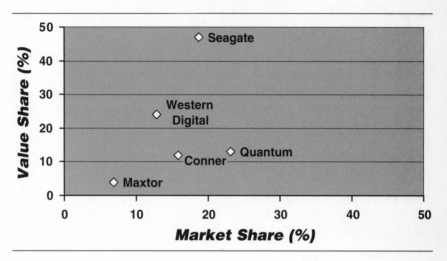

earnings exceeded those of the rest of the independent hard disk makers combined. It now had 600 engineers working on the design of disk drives for all its markets. Its advanced concepts group focused on research for developments that would be needed three to five years in the future. Its plant capacity exceeded 5 million square feet. It produced 50 disk drive models for 400 OEMs and distributors. It considered every market for disk drives and memory management to be its turf and every major enabling technology to be fodder for company advancement. Seagate's recipe for profit had become "get more new products to market in higher volumes more quickly than anyone else." Shugart also believed in rapid integration—as soon as the Conner deal closed, he gave the company five months to complete its integration.[15]

Quantum countered to some extent by buying DEC's disk drive division for $360 million to reinforce its own high-end business as DEC exited the industry. But Quantum had difficulties integrating the new operations,[16] and other companies such as IBM and Toshiba were driving up competitive pressures in its core markets. Quantum stayed close to Seagate in terms of market share, but Seagate's market cap was five times higher—the true mark of a market champion.

Shugart, along with Chuck Haggerty of Western Digital and other CEOs at the independent HDD makers, retired at the end of the 1990s. Seagate didn't appear to lose its course. It continues to develop products with industry-leading performance characteristics, continues to be among the first to introduce them to market, and claims to offer the industry's broadest range of disk storage products.

And Then There Were Three

Of the top five vendors in the market at the beginning of the 1990s, four—Seagate, Quantum, Western Digital, and Maxtor—were still in the game as the decade ended. The only major player that disappeared was Conner Peripherals, which had returned to the Seagate fold. In early 2000, Seagate, the acknowledged leader in total market share and market value, decided to merge with software firm Veritas. Its hard drive business was broken off and taken private by an investment group that planned to focus on market leadership rather than quarter-to-quarter results. Then, in late 2000, the newly profitable Maxtor made a dramatic move to capture market leadership as it announced it would buy Quantum Corporation's hard drive business for $2.3 billion in Maxtor stock. Based on second-quarter 2000 HDD sales, the newly merged Maxtor would have 31 percent of the market compared to 22 percent for Seagate. The old market champion, newly freed from quarterly financial pressures, would relish the challenge of recapturing its crown.

Aside from two inside mergers, why were there so few major changes in leadership in the past decade in such a dynamic, competitive market with annual generations of technology? Because the market leaders, tempered by crisis after crisis, had developed the ability to reinvent themselves as necessary via both technological and organizational innovation.

For many years, competition has been fiercest in the high-volume personal computer segment. It was here that Seagate perfected its rapid ramp-up and ramp-down capability to ensure quick entry and to avoid inventory buildups and resulting price wars. Ramp-up is now so fast that the best manufacturers can go from zero to millions of disk drives in a few months, enabling them to hit the market in force with minimum delay.[17] Every aspect of life in these companies is organized around the industry's crystal-clear critical success factors. Speed is high on that list. I once remarked to the HR director of Quantum that it was unusual for such a large company to not have a pension plan. He said, "No one here is really interested in pension plans, but let me tell you about the production line employee who got a $400,000 bonus for solving a problem that got us to market one month sooner."

Seagate's formula for enduring market leadership emphasizes a number of key themes. In contrast to mainstream management logic, it relies heavily on vertical integration to ensure capacity, quality, and control of frequent and rapid manufacturing changeovers. It has implemented aggressive cost reduction, quality, and cycle time disciplines throughout every aspect of its vertically integrated business structure. Seagate beats its larger competitors through speed and cost advantages, and steamrollers smaller rivals with scope, scale, and supply chain advantages as well as with targeted price wars.

The company also is very disciplined about its R&D efforts, maintaining a comprehensive portfolio of R&D projects but focusing its mobile development teams on short-term targets. Seagate's R&D approach is reminiscent of Alexander the Great's global conquest formula: It focuses on a specific target, brings massive force to the target, reduces it, and leaves a small force behind to oversee the new conquest while the main force moves on to the next walled city.

Seagate has built an extensive profile of products and services unmatched by anyone else in the industry. It competes in core commodity segments but also delivers a wide range of specialized solutions and applications to higher-margin market segments. These diverse revenue streams and margin sources strengthen Seagate for inevitable bruising price competition in commodity segments. Perhaps more than anything, however, Seagate vows never to be caught napping by the next generation of hard-drive data storage technology. If anything, it now forces the pace of development. Focused adherence to these principles has kept Seagate at the fore of perhaps the most hypercompetitive industry on the planet today. Seagate provides a powerful point of reference for all incumbent market leaders who wish to win reelection in their markets. Without such disciplines, incumbents will inevitably succumb to competitors who seize and deliver next-generation offerings. Table 5.1 lists some endurance lessons that can be learned from Seagate.

In late 2002, Seagate, its hard drive business split from software maker Veritas, returned to the public financial markets with a successful initial public offering (IPO) that valued the company at approximately $5 billion. Executing a successful high-tech IPO in 2002 put Seagate in very exclusive company. Meanwhile, market leader Maxtor was valued at less

Table 5.1
Endurance Lessons from Seagate

- Mobile development teams allow agile focus on next-generation offerings.
- Vertically integrate to control quality, cost, and capacity.
- Use aggressive cost-reduction disciplines.
- Be first to market with high volume (rapid ramp).
- Perfect transition disciplines.
- Use acquisitions to build profile.
- Possess a broad range of offerings.
- Beat smaller rivals with scope, scale, and price wars.
- Discourage larger competitors with cycle times.

than $1.5 billion. In the fourth quarter of 2002, Seagate reported quarterly revenue of $1.73 billion and profits of $198 million, up sharply from the prior year. In contrast, Maxtor's (plus Quantum's) revenues of $1.04 billion were down from a year earlier, and profits of $37.3 million were substantially below market champion Seagate's. The perennial market champion was back on top, stronger than ever.

The Mindset of a Market Champion

Seagate's experience provides powerful insights into the mindset of a market champion. Its competitive instincts and skills are highly developed. Seagate aggressively attacks insurgent competitors, frequently initiating price wars to limit their inroads, and accelerating cycle times to discourage entry by larger, established technology companies. Champion incumbents have a clear grasp on emerging developments in their markets and are quick to capture any innovations that affect their business. Seagate may not always be first to market with the latest technology, but it is typically first with high volume, high quality, and global availability for new offerings. It is quick to embrace and introduce any innovations in and around its core business, whether it be next generation hardware, software, application, or process technology.

The best incumbents are actively involved in the chaos zones that affect their industry. Microsoft has developmental alliances with some 3,000 software firms, giving it a close look at virtually all of the development activity underway in the packaged software industry. Promising new products in this industry will show up on Microsoft's screen at an early stage, allowing the firm to pursue acquisitions, distribution agreements, or parallel development projects. Although Microsoft is also active in the venture capital arena, its alliance program seems to provide a uniquely effective model for monitoring developmental activity in the extended software industry.

Cisco, in contrast, relies more heavily on its venture capital arm to participate in emerging technology sectors. It feeds investments into many promising technology companies and pounces aggressively on those that achieve technical breakthroughs, even prior to commercialization of the technology in some cases. Cisco has been widely lauded for its ability to identify, acquire, and integrate emerging technologies into its market leadership machine. Monitoring and capturing emerging innovations is key to success as a market champion, but there is more to the market champion's mindset.

One of the first responsibilities of any market leader is to ensure industry peace and prosperity. The leader must define and defend industry borders; that means establishing stable relationships with neighboring industries. Leaders must be particularly concerned about defending the industry's borders against substitute products and services, for example.

A second set of responsibilities fall upon the market leader as well. To ensure the health, well-being, and long-term survival of the industry, the leader must represent the industry's interest in political, legislative, and regulatory arenas, for starters. The leader will have to manage public relations for the industry and all aspects of government relations, areas that may have been ignored during the company's rise to power. As market leader, the champion should also shift its focus to primary demand for the industry's offerings. It is now the principal beneficiary of any increases in consumption of the industry's offerings and should do all in its power to increase generic demand. That may mean extending subsidies to emerging sources of demand through such efforts as providing equipment, grants, and other resources to the educational system, for example. Companies like IBM and Nortel have long been extremely active in supporting higher education in particular, both to familiarize new generations of technical talent with their offerings and to help stimulate and direct more students toward careers in their industries.

To a market leader, order and stability become paramount concerns. As an insurgent, the firm may have taken delight in disrupting the established order. Now it may become interested in minimizing disruption. As the main player in the market, it will desire to establish and enforce a stable competitive hierarchy. Disruptive activities, defined according to the champion's rulebook, become targets for punitive reactions. The incumbent's natural reaction to any disruptive development is not fight or flight, but attack or acquire, and perhaps more specifically, punish or purchase. The new champion must be concerned with all of the classes of competitors at work in its market, and it must develop strategies and tactics that limit inroads from any of these quarters.

The market champion must also look to the future—stagnation will set in if the firm is not continuously striving to improve its customer value proposition and modernize its offerings. Depending on the market environment, that may entail nothing more than consistent incremental improvements in elements of the customer's value proposition. In more dynamic environments, the market champion will need to define and pursue breakthroughs of its own. The champion's inevitable interest in order and stability may commute into resistance to change, and that must be avoided. Regardless of the environment, the market leader should embrace the responsibility for defining the industry's "road map" or migration path into the future. It is in the leader's very best interests to set the vision and direction for change and innovation in the industry, and it should aggressively embrace responsibility for setting current and future technology standards. Many market champions strengthen their hold on core industry platforms by creating complex architectures that incorporate a growing range of integrated components, elements, and offerings of the extended business community. Such architectures are a perfect manifestation of the urban community planning functions so central to the market champion's mindset.

A true market champion at its core is concerned about its extended community, competitive stability, customer and stakeholder value delivery, industry health and well-being, and the future state of the business it dominates. Emerging market champions in particular may wish to embrace this mindset as part of their path to primacy, just as enduring market champions retain some of the insurgent's mindset.

NOTES

1. Lori Liggett, "The Founders of Sears, Roebuck & Company," in *1890s America: A Chronology,* American Culture Studies department, Bowling Green State University Web site, 1997.

2. Statistical Service Center, Association of American Publishers, Feb. 16, 2000.

3. Joann Muller, "Can Borders Turn the Page?" *Business Week,* April 3, 2000, p. 75.

4. Based on trends for department store sales volume from the U.S. Department of Commerce Bureau of the Census, 1992–1997.

5. Theodore Levitt, "Marketing Myopia," *Harvard Business Review,* July–Aug. 1960, p. 45.

6. R. Mauborgne, Creating New Market Space, *Harvard Business Review,* Jan. 1999, p. 83.

7. Maury Wright, "The Disk Drive: Winner and Still Storage Champion," InfoAccess, Jan. 21, 1999.

8. See Christensen, Clayton M., *The Innovator's Dilemma: When New Technologies Cause Great Firms to Fail,* Harvard Business School Press, Cambridge, 1997, for a discussion of the disk drive industry.

9. Peter Nulty, "Big Memories for Little Computers," *Fortune,* Feb. 8, 1982, p. 50.

10. "The Disk-Drive Boom Has Suppliers Spinning," *Business Week,* Feb. 6, 1984, p. 68.

11. Brian O'Reilly and Lynn Fleary, "How Tom Mitchell Lays Out the Competition," *Fortune,* March 30, 1997, p. 90.

12. Lawrence M. Fisher, "Seagate Trips, Industry Cringes," *New York Times*, Aug. 23, 1988, p. D-1.

13. "Happy Days Again For Hard Disk Makers," *Investor's Business Daily*, May 20, 1994, p. A3.

14. Brian Deagon, "Executive Update; Competition," *Investor's Business Daily*, Oct. 22, 1993, p. 4.

15. Seagate 1995 Annual Report.

16. Peter Elstrom, "Why More Mergers May Hit Splintered Disk-Drive Field," *Investor's Business Daily*, Oct. 5, 1995, p. A8.

17. David McKendrick, "Hard Disk Drives," in *U.S. Industry in 2000: Studies in Competitive Performance,* 1999, The National Academy Press, pp. 287–328.

CHAPTER 6

ADVICE FOR INCUMBENTS

THE INNOVATIVE INCUMBENT

It is said that no revolution was ever led by the establishment—not true. Many established companies have achieved breakthroughs to transform themselves, renew old leadership positions, and create new value. Seagate was born and bred in Silicon Valley, and it may be difficult for the average Fortune 1000 firm to adopt its approach to constant innovation. Let us look then at the oldest, stodgiest company we can find, and talk about how it set world speed records in corporate transformation.

Transforming American Standard

Let's revisit American Standard of Piscataway, NJ, best known as a manufacturer of bathroom fixtures. Older than the old economy, American Standard has been a market leader in plumbing for over a century. Based

on the DFT breakthrough described in Chapter 1, it looks as if this an-
cient company will be a market champion for many years more.

American Standard's breakthrough originated in a financial crisis. Nothing more concentrates the mind than the prospect of demise. Emanuel
"Mano" Kampouris, American Standard's CEO, was faced with these
hard facts: external financing was unavailable; he would have to generate
cash from internal sources to service the company's debt payments or
hand over the company to its bondholders. The key, he decided, was to
reduce working capital and free those funds to service the debt. American Standard chose to introduce across the company an innovative supply
chain, manufacturing and order fulfillment approach called DFT. Drop-
ping the traditional approach of using demand forecasts to set production
schedules, the company shifted to manufacturing only in response to
customer orders. Simultaneously, the company worked to dramatically
reduce production cycle times and implement just-in-time techniques
across its supply chain. In one stellar example, the timeline for preparing
a master mold for a ceramic plumbing product was reduced to two days
from more than 80 days. The goal was radical reduction of raw-materials,
work-in-progress, and finished-goods inventories.

The DFT program was implemented across the enterprise—in its
global plumbing, air conditioning (Trane), and air brake (Westinghouse)
business segments. From 1988 to 1996, inventory turns increased from
2.8 to more than 11 times, and total working capital declined by over 50
percent. With the multidimensional advantages delivered by the DFT
breakthrough, American Standard is gaining market share in its three core
businesses, strengthening its position as the global leader in all three industries. The strength of its transformation can be seen on the company's
Web home page, where set in bold type and prominently positioned by a
photo of the planet is the following sentence: Our company grows
STRONGER every year, better able to OUTPERFORM industry
competitors. Demand Flow Technology is the foundation of our success."

American Standard typifies an innovative incumbent aggressive in recasting itself and its markets. It is imperative that incumbents either initiate or embrace the sources of innovation at work in their industry to renew growth, profits, and value; that will not happen if the firm is focused on incremental optimization of its current operations. Existing market champions intent on perfecting the present may be doomed to be displaced by a new generation of market leaders—those who champion the next-generation technologies, business models, and practices that reshape markets. Incumbents must lead the revolution that upsets the status quo if they are to remain market champions. Optimization strategies are unlikely to support sustained leadership in most businesses. Despite our admiration for Jack Welch and GE, we don't think it is yet the role model for corporate innovation, or even sustained value creation.

Optimization Strategies

Here are several examples of established incumbents who embraced the GE model. A premier example not only embraced the model but also employed a key GE executive to lead in executing it. After a lengthy stint as GE's vice chairman, working side-by-side in a virtual partnership with Jack Welch, Larry Bossidy vacated the post in 1991 to take the helm at faltering $12 billion AlliedSignal.

Setting up shop in AlliedSignal's Morristown, NJ, headquarters, the Massachusetts native went right to the GE playbook to bring the money-losing company out of the doldrums. The three key plays Bossidy executed were business-portfolio, performance-culture, and cost-cutting initiatives. With the strategy of focusing on AlliedSignal's aerospace and automotive businesses, he auctioned off assets and shuttered offices and factories. Bossidy also shook up AlliedSignal's senior management, reshuffling positions and retaining only those executives who were in tune with the new mission. To a senior management of 140 heads, he added a total of 40 outsiders. He sheared headcount by 18,000 positions to a total of 86,000 employees and consolidated the number of business units to 38 from 54.

Figure 6.1
The GE Playbook in Action at Allied Signal

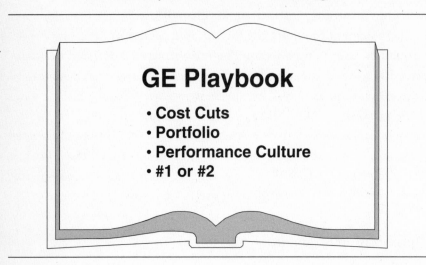

He also pushed the company to reduce the number of suppliers by two thirds, bringing the total down to a more manageable 3,000 vendors.

Á la GE, Bossidy strongly stressed the need for benchmarking and for executives to meet their targeted commitments. He was a rapid follower in implementing the "A" player executive development framework perfected at GE. And, in his first year at AlliedSignal, Bossidy took 86,000 people through a direct descendant of Welch's GE Workout development program.

Bossidy didn't see this as incremental change for AlliedSignal, by the way. Not at all—rather, he saw it as shooting for a "quantum jump." And for company management and employees, no doubt it certainly felt like one. AlliedSignal nearly tripled its market value by 1994, and net income soared well into the black. As Welch was doing over in New England, Bossidy also turned his efforts toward making AlliedSignal a global company.

Nonetheless, Larry Bossidy was unable to attain his key personal goal of building AlliedSignal from a $12 billion corporation into a $20 billion one. Growth does not normally follow from optimization efforts. A $10-billion hostile run at electrical-connector company AMP failed. With retirement looming in 2000 and no apparent successor in sight, Bossidy cut a $15 billion acquisition deal with Minneapolis landmark firm Honeywell. That deal got AlliedSignal over the $20 billion revenue mark. The upshot, however, was that AlliedSignal would sacrifice its corporate identity to the more recognizable Honeywell name.

After the December 1999 merger, Michael Bonsignore of Honeywell became CEO of the combined company. Using the playbook, aggressive cost-cutting and head-count reduction were underway across the company, and portfolio divestitures were planned. But a declining Euro piled onto the typical postmegamerger difficulties, and the new Honeywell missed its earnings targets. This earnings shock spooked investors, and Honeywell lost half its market value. Criticism from some quarters held that Honeywell had married a mediocre company, one more interested in massaging earnings than in long-term organic growth and that unless it got its act together the newly merged company could itself become an acquisition candidate.[1]

Those predictions proved accurate when, less than a year later, United Technologies attempted to acquire the firm for $40 billion. Seeing Honeywell in play, Jack Welch postponed his retirement plans and oversaw a $48 billion bid for the firm. Although GE and Honeywell had overlapping businesses in such areas as avionics, automated controls and chemicals, there were only a few overlapping products. GE's dominance of the aircraft engine and servicing market, for example, was nicely complemented by Honeywell's preeminence in commercial aircraft electronics and air traffic control systems. The fit in fact was too good for European antitrust regulators, who nixed the deal and sent Honeywell back into play, its future unfocused, its survival as an independent company very much in question. The GE playbook had led this company to an undesirable end zone.

Aetna, We Don't Get Ya

Other companies have implemented GE-type strategies in a more piece-meal fashion, sometimes successfully and other times with regrettable results. Another Connecticut company, multiline insurer Aetna Life and Casualty, embraced the GE model fervently but futilely. Like GE, Aetna sharpened its portfolio focus, sold a number of secondary businesses and used the proceeds to pursue market leadership in core industries, engaged in a series of facility closings, and attempted to downsize and get control of a massive cost structure. It aggressively refocused its portfolio along GE principles. Following the garage sale of its large but unprofitable property and casualty operation to Travelers Corporation, Aetna attempted to specialize and achieve leadership in the health insurance and HMO field. It spent $11 billion to purchase three HMOs in rapid succession, including the expensive New York Life health care unit ($1 billlion/$600 per member), the relatively cheap but financially troubled Prudential Health-Care ($1 billion/$200 per member) and the grossly overpriced US Health-care ($9 billion/$3,000 per member).[2]

Thus, aping Jack Welch's strategy of focusing on market leadership, Aetna became the nation's largest health insurer. Aetna's CEO Richard J. Huber boasted in 1998, "We are going to change the landscape of the whole industry." Meanwhile, consolidation across the health-care insurance industry had created an inner circle of three national insurers. (In addition to the freshly monikered Aetna US Healthcare, the others were Cigna Corporation and United Healthcare Corporation.) Aetna, long a laggard in making intelligent use of computers and information technology, faced the nearly impossible task of quickly integrating three huge and different information systems. In the field, Aetna's habitually heavy-handed cost-control and contracting methods proceeded to outrage and alienate many patients, hospitals, doctors, and the American Medical Association (AMA) itself, all in a high-profile manner. Apparently seeing neither the patient nor the physician nor the hospital as its customers,

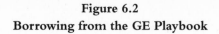

Figure 6.2
Borrowing from the GE Playbook

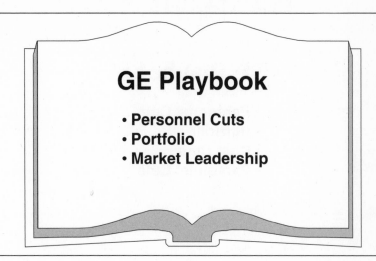

Aetna had placed all its bets on growing market share in a business in which for a variety of reasons it could not provide a reasonable return to another key constituency: its shareholders. Aetna's share price declined by 30 percent in 1999.

In early 2000, with shareholders outraged at the insurer's poor performance—and at Aetna's turning down a $10 billion takeover bid by Dutch insurer ING and Wellpoint Health Networks—Richard Huber resigned and was replaced by William H. Donaldson, who promised to separate the financial and health businesses. The company's market cap was below $8 billion when Aetna announced it would sell its financial services business. Aetna agreed to pay $82.5 million to disgruntled shareholders who claimed the firm misled them over the progress of its merger with US Healthcare. In late 2000, it sold its financial services and international operations to ING for $7.7 billion, after which it would emerge as purely a healthcare business.[3] Aetna's journey in the 1990s found no share of the glory that was GE—but it could have been worse.

Figure 6.3
Sunbeam's Game Plan

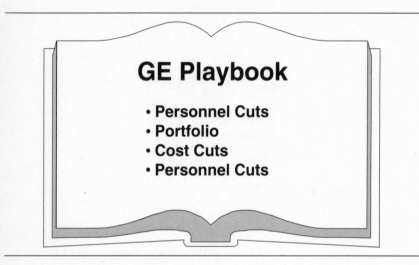

GE Playbook

- Personnel Cuts
- Portfolio
- Cost Cuts
- Personnel Cuts

Chainsaw Massacre

Another 1990s' optimization exercise makes AlliedSignal and Aetna look good. Rather than a protégé of GE's "Neutron" Jack Welch, this unfortunate consumer products company Sunbeam Corporation got "Chainsaw" Al Dunlap, a protégé of 1980s corporate raider Sir James Goldsmith. Having cut his teeth mostly in pulp and paper products companies, Dunlap was fresh from downsizing Scott Paper and selling it to competitor Kimberly-Clark.

A self-styled "Rambo in Pinstripes," Dunlap went at Sunbeam in 1996 with a ferocity that grabbed Wall Street's attention and hyped the firm's prospects, driving the share price from $12.25 to nearly $50 in late 1997. He fired 6,000 employees from the Boca Raton, Florida-based firm, eliminating half the company's jobs and cutting human resources staff from 75 to 17. He slashed an incredible 87 percent of Sunbeam's product lines. Rather than transforming the company's business and gaining the reward of a high and lasting value share, Dunlap slashed his way through Sunbeam's plants and people and used the short-term profits to buy a temporary stock high. In October 1997, the stock hit a record $50 a share.

But on April 3, 1998, as word hit Wall Street about possible improprieties in the company's accounting, Sunbeam suddenly became the most actively traded issue on the New York Stock Exchange—and not in a nice way. By the time the market closed, the high-flying firm's stock stood at $34.375, down nearly one fourth from what its value had been only that morning. Dunlap was ousted two months later by a chagrined board of directors, purportedly for failing to meet earnings projections. By April of 2000, the stock of the eviscerated Sunbeam was bumping along in the mid-single digits; a year later, it became a penny stock; and a year after that it disappeared from sight.

ACQUISITION STRATEGIES

The message is clear—don't rely on portfolio pruning, cost cuts, and optimization strategies to create value and certainly not to achieve renewal and growth. Nor should incumbents expect to renew themselves solely through acquisition. Unfortunately, most acquisitions have a sorry record. Harvard professor Michael Porter, a leading expert on competitive strategy, found that purchasers subsequently divested 58 percent of acquisitions in new industries.[4] The McKinsey consulting firm estimated that 60 percent of mergers fail financially.[5] PricewaterhouseCoopers studied 300 of the largest mergers during the 1990s and found that three years later, 57 percent of the merged firms' total shareholder return lagged their industry average.[6]

Crucial to the success of an acquisition is the issue of integration. Is the acquisition to be treated as a separate venture or incorporated into the fiber of the parent? For many companies, the challenge of how to integrate an acquisition is one of monumental proportions—one in which the issues of culture clash, employee redundancy, executive responsibility, and personal security distract mightily from the original purpose of the acquisition. It might be tempting, therefore, to leave the acquired company alone and avoid the question of integration entirely.

The Integration Imperative

Those companies for whom acquisitions are a healthy part of a balanced corporate diet tend to view things somewhat differently. Here, GE is a powerful role model. Take the example of GE Capital, a major financial services force with 27 separate businesses and more than 50,000 employees, which made hundreds of acquisitions worldwide in the last five-year period. GE Capital has made acquisition integration a distinct business function, charged with planning for the acquired firm's successful integration from the very first due diligence discussions, through and well beyond the completion of the purchase. Decisions about management structure, key roles, reporting relationships, layoffs, and so on are made and implemented as soon as possible after the deal is done.[7] Proactive, structured processes are critical to successful integration.

An Effective Substitute for R&D?

I believe the best acquisitions are "component" or "point" acquisitions—in other words, acquisitions where specific elements of a future business model or market profile are brought into the core organization. Strategy leads to acquisitions, not the other way around. In high-tech industries, such acquisitions can usefully serve as a substitute for certain R&D efforts. Cisco Systems has made a science of absorbing new technology and engineers via acquisition. Indeed, Cisco CEO John Chambers has constructed much of his senior management team with executives who have joined the company via acquisitions.[8]

Critics have charged that much of Cisco's heavy spending on R&D (13 percent of revenues) is used to integrate its acquired technologies rather than to develop new ones. A savvy observer might say that's just the ticket. "If we're going to lose the people who are important to the success of the startup company, we're probably not going to have an interest," said Dennis Powell, Cisco's controller.[9] So Cisco maintains a centralized team of 15 to 25 persons to handle integration even after an acquisition is completed.

Microsoft, which (like Cisco) has made something of a monthly habit of acquisitions, bought its way into the browser market when it was a late entrant. Neither Cisco Systems nor Microsoft is perfect, of course. Each has made its share of blunders in acquiring other companies. So you can easily imagine the challenge facing a firm that doesn't buy another company every few months—one that can't afford to have the odd merger head south.

Innovation in the Core

In his seminal book "The Innovator's Dilemma," Clayton M. Christensen contrasted incumbent companies' inability to exploit disruptive technologies with insurgents' success in leveraging such technologies for strategic advantage.[10] Christensen goes on to recommend that incumbents place innovative initiatives outside the corporate walls in order to give them the freedom and resources they need to grow. It is widely held that breakthroughs are best nurtured by spinning them off from the mother ship—that the self-contained venture will be clear of bureaucratic entanglements and cultural resistance and encouraged to grow in a hothouse garage environment.

I disagree. Are industry incumbents so incapable of originating and developing innovations that "out-of-body" ventures have become the only route to salvation?

Given the likelihood of failure for such ventures, a term more appropriate than *spin-off* might be *spinout*. Internally generated endogenic growth has more potential than the "out-of-body" exogenic growth—that is, growth by merger, spin-off, joint venture, and so on. Exogenic growth doesn't work, mostly. Why not? For starters, independent ventures forego the critical support and resources of the parent—particularly channels and customers—and much of the collective learning that would otherwise take place when a company enters a new business is lost. Neglect, even if it is benign, hampers growth. For breakthrough to be successful in the marketplace, all the company's talents and resources—not a few paratroopers—must be totally engaged in the effort. Paratroopers—spin-off teams—are suicide squads unless the main invasion force follows them into the targeted territories.

The success of the spin-off venture ultimately depends upon the core business it is positioned to displace. Access to resources, customers, capacity, and management attention are nutrients for growth. Denied them, the venture is likely to wither away.

ENDOGENIC GROWTH—PATHWAY TO BREAKTHROUGH?

Successful endogenic growth relies on one crucial factor—the ability of the existing organization to nurture and grow the next-generation business; this is no small feat. It is more common to find that the worst enemy of the company's future business is its present organization. It comes down to a simple question: "Is your organization like an adult crocodile, with an inherent tendency to devour its young, or is it more like a protective, supportive, nurturing mammal?" It is a question of how you treat the next generation. Success with endogenic growth stems from cultivating successful parenting instincts in what otherwise may be a harsh reptilian swamp.

The Principle of Successful Parenting

Here's the main point: Whether you intend to build innovation or buy it, integrating it into the core business and organization is the most effective way to grow successfully. This is what's meant by *endogenic* growth, and it's the best way to transform an established company. While attempting to achieve breakthrough endogenically puts the fledgling future business into the rough give-and-take of everyday corporate life, it nonetheless enables the firm to graft the new sapling directly to the family tree. The implications of that statement for obtaining support and maintaining morale, in current operations as well as for the success of the new venture, simply can't be overstated.

Exogenic growth sacrifices many of the valuable inputs obtainable from a company's roots—its first ring of suppliers, customers, and stakeholders. A business only succeeds by understanding and responding to its current and potential customers' requirements and expectations. The parent company can provide the new venture with an invaluable resource: its hard-won base of customers (not to mention the leverage of its existing marketing and sales structure). Although not every current customer may be a prospect for the new product or service, the lower cost and effort required to cross-sell current customers compared with prospecting for, attracting, and closing new ones can mean the difference between success and failure. Furthermore, select customers can serve as inexpensive yet invaluable advisors and beta test sites during product design and development. Later on, they can serve as highly visible early adopters during rollout. The process can even help to enhance customer relationships for the company's existing lines of business.

Where would IBM be today if it had spun out its software businesses to develop its own customer base? Would it generate more than 50 percent of its profits from services today if it had not tightly integrated services into its core business and organization? IBM shows the power of integrating new growth vectors directly into the core of the current business and organization.

Integration was central to Schwab's success as well. In 1995, Schwab created e.Schwab, an independent division focused on the web. By 1996, some 800,000 investors had gone online to do their trading. But as e.Schwab grew quickly, so did customers' frustrations. "It was confusing and kludgy," Schwab recalls. "It wasn't Schwab-like in its customer focus. It was obvious that customers didn't feel good about the non-integrated services." Schwab and David Pottruck, co-chief executive, faced a tough decision: Should they keep e.Schwab separate or merge it into the company's mainstream services?

Truly integrating the services meant reducing trading fees to *all* customers to $30—a move that executives estimated could cost the firm $100 million a year in lost revenues, for starters. Furthermore, added expenses would result from allowing Web users full access to all 290 of Schwab's branch offices and all the company's customer service representatives. Then there were the costs of creating online capacity and free Web trading workshops for those regular customers who would now choose to use the Internet, cannibalizing existing trading commissions. But Schwab didn't hesitate. "We had risked the position of the company any number of times," Schwab says. It had sacrificed hefty amounts of potential revenue in 1992 when it introduced no-fee IRAs and debuted no-load mutual funds. "They were huge risks, but we thought they were better for the customers," he says. So was online trading, and Schwab would develop this initiative as aggressively as it had explored all the other paths to self-service securities trading. In 1998, Schwab reintegrated e.Schwab back into the company, coupling it intimately with its traditional brokerage services. Online brokerage went from a separate line of business to an integral part of the company's operations. In one year, online accounts doubled and total customer accounts rose to more than 5.5 million. David Pottruck, Schwab's president, termed the transformation nothing short of "spectacular."[11] Integration was the magic ingredient.

Successful incumbents focus close to the core and far from the quo. The most powerful formula for sustainable market leadership flows directly from combining innovation and integration. Moreover, enduring market champions embrace the role and the responsibilities of leaders who are here to stay. The most fundamental of these imperatives is to seize the sources of change in the market and integrate them forcefully into the existing core business.

NOTES

1. Neal St. Anthony, "Honeymoon's Over," *Minneapolis Star Tribune,* July 9, 2000, p. 1D.

2. Milt Freudenheim, "Fiercer Aetna Sets Its Sights on Dominating Health Care," *New York Times,* Dec. 14, 1998, p. C1.

3. "Shareholder Settlement to Cost Aetna $82.5M," *New York Daily News,* Sept. 27, 2000, p. 37.

4. Porter, M. E., "From Competitive Advantage to Corporate Strategy," *Harvard Business Review,* May/June, 1987, pp. 43–49.

5. *McKinsey Quarterly,* Winter, 1998, No. 1, pp. 56–66.

6. M. A. Donnellan, W. Likhit, and D. J. Price, Foresight on the Web Newsletter, PricewaterhouseCoopers, January 1999, http://www.indiainitiative.com/foresightnew/jan1999/fsindex.htm

7. R. N. Ashkenas, L. J. DeMonaco, and S. C. Francis, "Making the Deal Real: How GE Capital Integrates Acquisitions," *Harvard Business Review,* Jan.–Feb., 1998, pp. 165–177.

8. A. Reinhardt, "Meet Cisco's Mr. Internet," *Businessweek Online,* Sept. 13, 1999, http://www.businessweek.com

9. G. Donnelly, "Acquiring Minds: Cisco and Lucent Buy into the Telecom Revolution with Strategies that Clash—and Converge," *CFO Magazine,* Sept. 1999.

10. Clayton M. Christensen, *The Innovator's Dilemma: When New Technologies Cause Great Firms to Fail,* Harvard Business School Press, Cambridge, 1997.

11. Schwab 1998 Annual Report.

CHAPTER 7

AIM, READY, FIRE

Focus: *A Latin word for the altar in the Roman home at which the family gods were worshipped*

SUCCESSFUL BREAKTHROUGHS tend to follow a generic pattern. Quite simply, enterprise leaders seize control of the organization's attention, establish a clear, actionable agenda, and forcefully focus the firm's resources on an outrageous objective and a specific set of implementation priorities. The modus operandi practiced by successful breakthrough firms can generally be described as *aim, ready, fire*. They establish a clear target and specific initiatives, align the organization, provide implementation structure and resources, and manage execution in a focused and systematic manner. Here are the key elements:

1. *Aim:* Develop a vision that identifies the organization's collective ambition; describe the future state to be achieved and define a highly articulated plan of action to achieve that ambition.
2. *Ready:* Align the organization. Communicate extensively to focus, engage, and inspire the team. Create contracts with key team

members. Allocate resources, assign responsibilities, and create program and performance management infrastructure.

3. *Fire:* Focus resources on executing a specific implementation agenda. Intervene in breakdowns, reward accomplishments, communicate results, and reinforce progress.

Although there are many variables, some version of this approach underlies all the successful breakthrough firms we observed. One variation on this theme deserves mention. In some cases, breakthrough strategies emerged *after* a discrete innovation had already occurred. Leadership then seized on the broader strategic potential of the innovation to recast the company's business model and drive toward more ambitious objectives. Firms who "discover" a breakthrough engine in their midst may opportunistically leverage a discrete innovation into a broader breakthrough in profile, market position, and financial performance. Here is one such example.

Vons, a Southern California grocery chain, was the pioneer in the deployment of point of sale (POS) scanners at checkout counters in the 1970s, introducing the then-embryonic technology long before other retailers did. That head start, as we shall see, has allowed Vons the first crack at a rich set of 21st-century business opportunities. First, let's look at how a discrete process innovation evolved into a broader business breakthrough. Scanners expedite checkout and enable improved inventory turns, freeing up valuable space in the front and back of the store. This "found space" can be added to the selling area or subtracted from the lot size, thereby improving returns on expensive California real estate. Scanners also drive reductions in labor cost and improvements in customer service. The key to these benefits was accelerating *transaction velocity* in the checkout process. Focusing on operating excellence, Vons's management became obsessed with finding ways to speed up the process.

This obsession led Vons to identify and address possible sources of delay at the checkout counter, such as coupon processing and payment by check. More than 500 billion coupons were printed and distributed in the United States last year; fortunately, fewer than ten billion were redeemed. Processing of coupons at the checkout counter can be a time-consuming and costly exercise. Scanners provided an ideal solution to the coupon-processing problem. Virtually all coupons today contain bar codes, and the coupons can be scanned at the checkout counter. The system will determine whether the coupon is still valid and whether the product specified on the coupon was part of the customer's purchase. Credits can be automatically deducted from the customer's bill, and back-office processing of the coupons can also be automated. Today, almost all grocers use systems similar to those pioneered by Vons more than twenty years ago.

Scanners could have been used to help solve the check payment problem as well, but it proved more difficult to gain acceptance for adding bar codes on checks, and credit cards were not yet an option. Vons elected to address the payment problem with another technology, installing online card readers at each checkout counter in the late 1980s. Customers were provided with VonsChek cards that they could swipe for automated approval of check-writing privileges. The use of these online card readers, combined with scanners, dramatically reduced delays at the checkout counter. Transaction velocity was accelerated, thereby reducing the number of counters and cashiers necessary and improving customer service. These technologies are now standard fare in Vons and other grocery stores, but Vons's early lead in their use in the 1970s and 1980s led to a significant breakthrough in its business model.

Vons's obsession with accelerating the checkout process and its investments in advanced technologies led not only to multiple operating benefits, but it also created a spectacular set of new business growth opportunities. Although the sole motive for deploying these advanced technologies was to drive operating excellence at the checkout counter, the primary benefit was new growth opportunities. The scanner and card reader added to each checkout counter not only increased the speed, efficiency, service level, and accuracy of the process, but they also captured valuable information that could be used in a variety of ways to enhance Vons' business. Some of these benefits flowed from *turbocharging* the data captured at the point of sale and recycling it to improve purchasing, inventory management, and shelf-space optimization. New profits appeared from selling POS data to third parties. Market research firms paid $3,000 to $4,000 per month per store for bulk POS data, allowing Vons to generate annual incremental revenue of more than $10 million from its more than 300 stores. But far bigger opportunities were exposed by this innovation at the checkout counter.

While POS scanners provided useful aggregate information about product movements, the online card reader at each checkout station added a vital information element to the equation. These card readers, introduced to validate customers' check-writing privileges, gave Vons the ability to identify their customers at the time and point of sale. That information was then matched with scanner data to identify individual customers' purchasing patterns with a level of precision previously unimaginable.

This new level of precision added enormous value to Vons's data stream; this value could be exploited in a number of ways. The knowledge base could be used to support a sophisticated mailing list business, for example. Vons could also use its newfound customer knowledge to promote the sales of its private-label products with individualized promotional incentives. Vons could assist market research firms or consumer product companies in identifying customer responses to new products, promotions, packaging changes, and pricing initiatives in far more depth and detail than was previously possible.

Vons chose to focus most of its growth efforts on a new direct marketing service for VonsClub members. VonsClub upgraded the initial Chek card with a frequent buyer program. At checkout, customers swiped their cards and automatically received discounts on specially marked

Club promotions. Their receipt informed them how much money they saved, and points accumulated toward free prizes. Vons also introduced a "lottery" feature that turned the swiping of the card into the equivalent of pulling the handle on a slot machine.

Club members receive mailings of promotions and coupons specially tailored to their individual buying patterns. Redemption rates for these tailored coupons can run ten times higher than do those of traditional coupon programs, and vendors who use this system report significant and sustained increases in revenue following a targeted distribution.

Vons's direct marketing unit contributed more than half of Vons's total profits in its first full year of operation and may represent an even more important part of the company's future. Direct marketing is now a $80 billion business per annum in the United States, exceeding spending on TV advertising. As more precise customer information allows for better targeting of customers and as communication costs decline with the growth of online network services, direct marketing activity will increase dramatically. Vons is in a position to be a leader in the provision of the critical information needed by direct marketers for successful targeting of customers. This business opportunity is inherently more promising and profitable than is grocery retailing in Southern California, and Vons is in a strong position to capitalize on it. Others saw the value of Vons's breakthrough as well. Old-school grocer Safeway acquired Vons in 1996 for $45 per share, tripling its share price.

Vons did not set out to transform itself into a direct marketing services company. Its obsession with operating excellence led to a performance innovation it could leverage into a broader business breakthrough. Was it a matter of luck? I think not. Their obsession with operating excellence almost ensured that they would be the first to realize the potential of new technologies in their business. In much the same way, Charles Schwab's early adopter mentality and obsession with customer service ensured that it would be the first to discover the power of the Internet in the brokerage business. But early adoption alone is not sufficient to achieve a business breakthrough. The aim, ready, fire cycle still applies. Leadership must create a focused plan that exploits new capabilities to achieve outrageous objectives.

CRISIS AND INNOVATION

Not all firms are so fortunate as to find a breakthrough racehorse in their barn. More typically the breakthrough cycle begins of necessity. At American Standard, Caterpillar, IBM, Mervyns, Progressive, Plains Cotton Cooperative, and more, the continued survival of the firm required fundamental transformation. In many cases, the process begins with a search for the core strategy that will save the firm and start a new success cycle. At both American Standard and Caterpillar, for example, formal "study" groups scoured the planet, benchmarking state-of-the-art sites and searching for the performance driver to fuel their transformation and renewal. Both firms drew heavily from the Toyota manufacturing system, with American Standard even employing a group of retired Toyota industrial engineers to help shape its demand flow technology initiative.

Caterpillar's Plant With a Future (PWAF) program began when executive vice president (EVP) Pierre Guerindon assembled a cross-functional team of 16 program managers who were sequestered and told to formulate the PWAF vision. That team traveled out into the global arena and documented best practices in manufacturing. They emerged with what was referred to as the Factory 2000 document, which outlined best manufacturing practices worldwide. Many sources of information were used: numerous consultants, benchmark companies, manufacturing associations, and so on. From this work the team formulated an end-to-end vision of continuous-flow manufacturing, supported by fully integrated information systems and advanced technologies that would dramatically improve operating performance in multiple dimensions, create new capability, and renew the venerable earth-moving machinery maker. That PWAF vision became the *aim* of Caterpillar's transformation strategy. Guerindon described the vision:

> The goal is continuous, synchronous work flow. Continuous— meaning no accumulation of inventory—no interruptions—no dropping the ball. And synchronous—meaning it all runs like a ballet. Parts and components are delivered on time, in the proper sequence, exactly to the point where they're needed.[1]

Explicit in Caterpillar's vision were a series of ambitious goals. These goals included concrete operating metrics, as well as qualitative milestones and new capabilities, such as the following:

- Zero idle inventory
- Mass customized products manufactured on a build-to-order basis
- Global visibility of the total supply chain
- Supplier participation in product and process design
- Implementation of total quality control
- Electronic procurement
- Lower lead times on customer shipments

Caterpillar's PWAF team created a carefully crafted, highly architected strategy for implementation across the company. PWAF was articulated into 77 very specific production and assembly processes. These 77 bundles, as they were called, formed a central repository of best practices that could be accessed by Caterpillar plant managers. Introduced to the manufacturing community at a semiannual manufacturing managers' gathering, plant managers were given a mandate to develop plans to begin implementing PWAF bundles in their facilities. The 16 members of the core team were dispersed as consultants to help factory heads identify priority opportunities for implementing bundles that would substantially improve performance at their location.

Pierre Guerindon, who had control of the entire capital budget for the company, reviewed all PWAF proposals personally. Plans of more than $10 million required Board approval as well. Each project was reviewed numerous times by Guerindon, and his questioning of alternatives could be "quite painful" if a plant manager was unprepared.

Guerindon's guidance was crucial. Tom McMahill, who worked between Guerindon and the factory managers assisting them in formulating their PWAF systems plans, remarked, "Personally, if you didn't have a person up there with that much drive and leadership, it would not have happened . . . it was too painful and the culture had to change too much."[2]

Virtually all plants worldwide were affected by PWAF. One plant manager put it the following way: "You had to participate, that was the only way to get capital funding."

Implementation of PWAF involved hundreds of local initiatives using the 77 best practice modules, which were closely tied to the overall architecture of PWAF. Caterpillar's performance gains were dramatic. Many impressive examples of PWAF projects at individual plants can be cited. At Caterpillar's Joliet Transmission complex, among other gains, PWAF innovations reduced total floor space by more than one million square feet. That found space became relevant as CAT soon concluded it would begin "insourcing" the production of key components, because its new manufacturing system would deliver the goods at lower cost, higher quality, and shorter lead times than its outside suppliers could match. Here are some aggregated results from the first five years of the program:

Inventory levels	-60%
Customer delivery lead times	-93% (145 days to 10 days)
In-plant defects	-85%
Warranty payments	-40%

New product introduction time	-70% (5 years to 18 months)
On time delivery performance	+70%
Product line	150 plus custom units

Caterpillar created a very specific vision of its preferred future state as a 21st-century manufacturing organization, with an overall architecture for that future state and highly articulated individual initiatives. That aim was then implemented in a highly focused fashion, with tight control of resources and high levels of accountability for plant managers. With successful implementation of PWAF, Caterpillar ended a downward spiral that began in the 1980s and solidified its position as market champion in its global market.

Caterpillar represents a classic aim-driven breakthrough strategy that began with a business crisis. Almost all breakthroughs by incumbents fall into this category. IBM and American Standard stand out as other notable examples; these are firms whose very existence was threatened. Is it necessary for a firm to face death before it can transform itself? No; but it helps if the specter can be visualized. John Gaulding, who led ADP's automated claim services (ACS) division through an extraordinary transformation, told us how he magnified bad news to create an atmosphere of crisis in his organization. ADP at the time had reported the longest string of consecutive quarterly earnings increases in corporate history. It was not a company concerned for its survival.

As Good as New at ADP

Yet, ADP's insurance claim services business was very much at risk. Wedded to a traditional mainframe-computing platform, its business model was highly vulnerable to attack by next-generation technologies boasting dramatically lower costs and enhanced capabilities. Still, recognition of this threat in itself was not sufficient to motivate action. New-wave competitors were emerging, but ADP retained its dominant market share in the insurance claims services business. Then in one single five-day period, three key customers left ADP to sign with emerging competitors. That event was the turning point in ACS's trans-formation.

Armed with data that showed rising market share for its new competi-tors and significant cost and capability advantages for the next-generation technology, Gaulding and chief operating officer (COO) Gerhard Blend-strup initiated a new strategy cycle. They created client teams that brought together sales, marketing, and technical personnel under the leadership of key executives to identify and respond to changing customer needs. Using this input and a new technology strategy that explicitly moved the company away from mainframes to a next-generation platform, ACS be-gan to develop a vision for the future. That vision projected a complete transformation of automotive insurance claims processing. Claims esti-mators would be enabled to calculate repair costs in the field quickly and precisely, using portable electronic tools to specify optimal repair proce-dures and locations, parts lists, and standard labor times, for starters. ACS's vision included a master database with interactive, electronic computer-aided design (CAD) templates for all vehicles, replacing the traditional mechanical drawings that served as repair estimation work-sheets. The database would be made available to adjusters in the field over mobile computing and communication platforms with an easy-to-use graphical user interface. Interactive pen-based tools would dramatically increase the productivity and quality of estimating repair costs. ACS's new system, called Audapoint, was an extraordinarily ambitious vision for the future of claims processing. It included a master file of standard labor times on any repair job on any vehicle, providing insurance com-panies a mechanism for managing repair shop costs. It also included elec-tronic access to a national parts exchange network to facilitate purchase and delivery of the correct parts for a repair job, reducing parts costs, lo-cal inventory holdings, and repair cycle times. The vision included a so-phisticated system for measuring repair shop performance as well.

ACS's vision was nothing less than a total transformation of the auto insurance claims and repair industries. It included a complete architecture for the industry's infrastructure and a new set of processes for claims estimation and auto repair management. That vision contained a series of specific initiatives, starting with the master database.

In order to make the transition to that new vision, Gaulding had to do several things. First, he had to convince his own organization to embrace the vision, and second, he had to sell the vision in the marketplace. Gaulding used biweekly town hall meetings with his employees to communicate the vision and rally the troops around his breakthrough strategy. Because of the extraordinary shift from mainframe systems to next-generation workstations, applications, and electronic platforms, Gaulding decided to repopulate his organization with new employees to bring fresh skills and perspectives into the organization. A new wave of employees, all very comfortable with the new technology platforms, helped tip the organization to embrace the new vision.

To freeze the marketplace until ADP could deliver on its vision, ACS created a compelling videotape that showed prototypes of the new technologies and processes in action. The videotape demonstrated how insurance companies could dramatically increase the productivity and performance of claims estimation, significantly reduce auto repair costs, and improve service to their customers. Of course, the tools shown in the videotape were not yet available. Nonetheless, the visualization of these new offerings was so compelling and credible, it allowed ADP to convince its customers to wait in selecting next-generation services until its new offerings were available. The video vision effectively froze emerging competitors in their tracks.

With a clear aim, a compelling vision, and a highly articulated transformation plan, Gaulding had readied his organization and the market for breakthrough and was able to focus on executing the breakthrough strategy. Implementing the vision required extraordinary effort. For example,

ACS purchased the services of every available AutoCad professional for a period of about a year and a half to convert mechanical drawings for 1,300 automobiles into electronic CAD files for its master database. ACS also hired several hundred software developers to create its new Auda-point estimating system. AudaPoint is their portable, pen-based estimating system that quickly generates repair requirements, part numbers and prices, and labor hours for repair work in the field. AudaPoint, later re-branded PenPro, also produces personalized settlement letters, parts lists, repair work orders, management reports, check drafts for payments to customers or repair shops in the field, and more. ACS also introduced its Shop Link service, which enables electronic transmission of repair estimations and digitized images directly to repair shops or insurance companies for claims approval.

Although much of ACS's vision required substantial internal systems development, it also made an important acquisition, picking up Hollander Services, who developed the standard numbering system for repair parts in the salvage industry. Hollander's Electronic Data Exchange Network (EDEN) system utilizes these interchange codes to find parts in distributor and salvage yard inventories across North America. Through EDEN, users can electronically locate parts and disseminate their own inventory information to other users. Hollander's inventory management system links more than 1,200 parts suppliers, allowing automated location, purchasing, and delivery of specific parts.

ACS's core database and automated estimation tools are now used to write more than 6 million estimates annually in the United States—more than half the total. ACS has gone on to introduce a score of services for insurance companies and body shops, as this establishment company leads the revolution in auto repair. And it did not stop there. It has taken its core breakthrough strategy to new markets as well. ACS, now renamed the Claims Management Solutions Division, today provides a variety of similar services in the medical claims market, an even larger business much in need of transformation. Still dwarfed by its larger sister divisions, Claims Management Solutions may be a much larger part of ADP's future.

ACS's success in transforming itself before the real crisis hit occurred to a great extent because the parent corporation had the foresight to bring in an experienced change leader in the person of John Gaulding. Transformation at ACS fundamentally followed the aim, ready, fire framework. Gaulding's sophisticated approach to transformation was central to this success story. A highly innovative West Coast executive in an Eastern establishment firm, Gaulding ultimately moved on to other challenges but not before triggering the transformation of ACS.

AIM, READY, FIRE IN ACTION

Breakthroughs can occur within freestanding divisions when the right local leadership and support from corporate come together. Here's another example of divisional transformation using the aim, ready, fire approach. Franklin Publishing (literary pseudonym), a midsized publisher of university textbooks, concluded in the mid-1990s that traditional textbooks were a dying industry. Unit sales were declining in the face of student resistance to rising prices (a college text can now easily exceed $100), faculty demands for fresher material (time to market for a new text was well in excess of one year), and the impact of new media teaching methods and materials.

Franklin's CEO assembled a core team of senior executives and led them through an assessment of the company's options. After extensive study and deliberation, the team crafted a new vision that called for the firm to remake itself as "a leading provider of electronic multimedia educational content and services." That vision was developed in detail and then deconstructed to identify 114 necessary elements. Using a backcasting technique, the 114 elements were integrated into a time-line sequence of 86 core projects. A program management office was established, led by the firm's COO, and project owners and members were assigned for each project. A specific implementation sequence was defined, and individual projects were executed in an orderly fashion.

The very first project focused on upgrading the old business model while building key capabilities needed in the future state. The firm implemented a digital textbook production system that bypassed traditional editorial and chemical-based graphics and typesetting editorial processes, cutting time to market by more than 75 percent. The economics of the new production line also allowed for smaller print runs and repair replenishment, reducing the risk of new projects and dramatically reducing inventory levels.

The new digital line dramatically improved the performance of the traditional business, with fresher materials for faculty and students, quicker time to market for authors, and lower costs and risks for the publisher. It also built a core capability necessary in a subsequent project—custom textbook publishing. Combined with its new digital content repository, the publisher was able to introduce the concept of custom textbooks to its faculty customers, allowing them to assemble separate chapters, articles, case studies, and other material into "textbooks" designed, titled, and authored by the professor. The firm's intent is to move beyond custom textbooks to custom educational packages, designed online.

Within two years of dedicated implementation effort, this company had built the core of its future business while dramatically improving the growth rate and profitability of its traditional business. It had positioned itself as the leading contender for market leadership in the era of electronic education and was moving rapidly to achieve that position when it was acquired by McGraw-Hill, the incumbent market leader. In less than three years Franklin had grown from less than 10 percent of McGraw-Hill's market share to over 20 percent, establishing itself as the innovative insurgent in the textbook market. McGraw-Hill apparently saw the power of Franklin's breakthrough and acquired it to secure their leadership position.

Franklin's leadership crafted and embraced a grounded vision for transformation, converted that vision into a specific program of action, readied the organization, and executed crisply to plan, with no diversions or delays. As a result, it was one of three firms we encountered who successfully implemented a breakthrough in less than three years. The aim, ready, fire framework was central to their success.

At both ADP and Franklin, an emerging market crisis was the catalyst for change. Crisis is the ally of the breakthrough leader. John Gaulding magnified the bad news to attack the complacency and lethargy he found at ACS and to build motivation for change. His advice might be, "If you don't have a crisis, create one!" But crisis is not a necessary prerequisite for breakthrough. Here's how a firm with a track record of successful growth used the aim, ready, fire framework to leap to the next level in its market.

NextLeap

UTi Worldwide is a fast-growing global logistics company. From humble origins in 1993, the company had grown from a basic freight-forwarding business in a handful of countries to a global network with operations around the world. In less than a decade, it had built a freight-forwarding network comparable in coverage to the largest players in the industry, with gross revenues in excess of $1 billion. In June of 2001, UTi's senior leaders gathered at Ye Olde Bell Inn outside London to reflect on their achievements and consider the future.

The mood was not one of impending crisis. The biggest issue of concern to the attendees was the intent of the company's three founders, Roger MacFarlane, Peter Thorrington, and Tiger Wessels, who rotated in the positions of chairman, CEO, and president. Were they perhaps considering a sale of the company now that it was a credible competitor? Or did they have plans to push on? The U.K. meeting was another "bardo" event—a transition period pregnant with possibilities. UTi had achieved its original strategic intent—what would come next? These questions were answered conclusively as the founders challenged the senior team to tackle a new outrageous objective.

Building a global freight forwarding network was UTi's first leap. For its next leap, UTi targeted a new outrageous objective. This second leap was designed to expand the company's portfolio of service offerings from freight forwarding and customs brokerage to a full line of supply-chain services and solutions. UTi's aim was to become the primary logistics partner for its customers, providing supply-chain solutions to global customers. Over the next few months, UTi's senior team polished their ambitions into a specific aim.

UTi's team formally utilized the aim, ready, fire framework to shape and execute the NextLeap strategy. Its aim focused on the journey from global freight forwarding to integrated logistics solutions, emphasizing its intended role as the primary logistics partner with key global customers. This aim, or preferred future state, was to be achieved through six core initiatives and a series of enterprise projects. Global teams, each led by senior executives, tackled planning for each of the six core initiatives, identifying key elements and articulating a plan of action in each area.

NextLeap was formally introduced to the company's top 100 executives at UTi's annual global network meeting held in South Africa in September 2001. With a concerted effort from its senior leaders, UTi had articulated its aim in just three months. At the meeting, each executive was equipped with a briefing kit, including a presentation to share with their employees. The CEO's office formally followed up to ensure that each country manager held a briefing session with their employees to prepare them for NextLeap. Multimedia CDs and tool kits were distributed three months later to facilitate further engagement. The company's new Intranet was widely used to disseminate information about NextLeap. Following four months of intensive communication and preparation, the fire phase of NextLeap began on February 1, 2002. UTi's NextLeap support office had been working diligently during the ready phase to prepare a set of high-priority enterprise projects for launch and execution. These projects were selected by the Senior Leadership Team from the list identified during articulation of the six core initiatives.

One of the first enterprise projects implemented at UTi was the global deployment of an "order management system" that enabled UTi to provide global visibility to its customers on specific shipments and subshipments. Visibility for warehouse inventory holdings was addressed in a later project. Other key projects focused on next-generation information systems. Another focused on defining, deploying, and delivering customer-specific standard operating procedures for global clients. Additional service offerings and infrastructure elements were in the pipeline, as part of an integrated master plan for migration to the new business model. Acquisitions were also treated as enterprise projects. Within the year, key acquisitions of contract logistics companies in Spain and the United States were completed, opening the door for delivery of end-to-end logistics services.

Although new service offerings and new customer relationships focused UTi's development activities, the primary purpose of NextLeap was more fundamental. Roger MacFarlane spoke frequently of "the podium." UTi believed that it had qualified for the global logistics Olympics with their first leap. Now they wanted to stand on the podium as a medal winner. At the end of 2002, as UTi approached the first anniversary of the launch of its NextLeap effort, Roger MacFarlane sent a brief memo to the company's strategic leadership team:

> On December 13th, UTi's market value was greater than Airborne Express, Tibbett and Britten, Kintetsu, Neptune Orient Line (which owns APL Shipping, APL Logistics and GATX), Forward Air, Pacer International, Eagle, and i2 Technologies (all had been well ahead of UTi a year earlier). Also on that day, UTi' market value was half that of Kuehne and Nagel (the world's largest ocean freight for-

warder), and three quarters the value of Pittston, which owns Brinks and BAX Global. (UTi's founders had departed BAX Global in the early 1990s). You can each be proud of your contribution to putting UTi into the Olympics of logistics. There are some competitors still ahead of us in the game: EXEL, Expeditors, Stinnes, and Nippon, so we can remain motivated as we think about the podium at the end of the NextLeap journey.

Just a few weeks earlier, UTi's global strategic leadership team had assembled at a beach hotel in Los Angeles for an annual strategy review. The team had last been together a year earlier to announce the launch of NextLeap. The difference in attitude was striking. In the 2002 meeting, management confidence and alignment were quantum levels higher than they were the year before. The core premises and paths of the NextLeap strategy were now proven and playing out as planned.

It is a wonderful feeling to be in a room with a group of global executives who are of one mind and one gut about common direction, priorities, and endeavors. It does not happen easily or often. As with any team, there were differing levels of commitment to the new strategy at the outset. NextLeap lived on shaky ground for a period of time. CEO Roger MacFarlane went to the mat on several occasions to ensure that key elements of the NextLeap strategy did not die on the vine. Financial and operating pressures were severe during this period; international trade volumes actually declined for the first time in modern history in 2002, and pressures from Wall Street were intense. There was overwhelming pressure to focus exclusively on short-term operations and financial results and to set aside the long-term strategy. For example, as UTi launched its first wave of enterprise projects, each project was staffed with a team of leaders from across the global network. Launch involved a week or more of in-depth team activity in the United States, followed by a significant commitment of time for up to six months. In staffing these projects, the very best and brightest members of the UTi organization were selected. Pulling them away from the core business at this point in time was a very painful exercise. There was also reluctance simply to pay the travel expenses for participants from around the world. Operating managers were being asked to dig down deep to reduce costs and hit operating and financial targets at the same time that their best people were being pulled out of the line, and they were being hit with significant travel expenses. The strain was intense. It was a real possibility that NextLeap would be relegated to standby status.

How did they stay the course? It is perhaps significant that at the NextLeap launch in South Africa in 2001, approximately one hundred members of the global leadership team were asked to select a theme for the NextLeap journey. UTi's senior executives had already chosen the theme of achieving outrageous objectives. However, the global leadership team rejected that phrase and chose instead the phrase *our clear commitment*. It was that commitment that pulled UTi through the precarious launch and ensured that NextLeap would take root and flourish. Roger MacFarlane put it the following way:

> When we first launched NextLeap, many people inside and outside the company said that it was impossible and couldn't be done. Yet, here we are just one year later, well on our way to achieving all of our objectives in an extremely difficult operating environment, and we've only just begun.

As UTi began the second year of its NextLeap journey, that clear commitment had been cemented by strong operating results and strategic progress. It was also obvious that UTi had created a new core competency—the ability to define, launch, and execute global enterprise initiatives and projects. UTi was becoming an integrated global enterprise, unified around a core breakthrough strategy. The aim, ready, fire framework served as the bridge to their destination.

FOLLOW A FRAMEWORK

Business engineering lies at the heart of breakthrough. Corporate and market transformation requires a critical mass of design and engineering effort. The previous examples reveal in-depth, systematic methods for large-scale enterprise innovation. Each used a highly structured framework to manage their transformation.

Big breakthroughs—those that transform firms and markets—are not discrete point innovations. Firms who tend to succeed at this game do not exhibit the same bias for action often associated with excellent companies. Entrepreneurial firms tend to fire frequently on all cylinders and in all directions. Breakthrough companies design highly architected plans and models for business transformation. They then act in a highly focused and systematic fashion to implement their designs. The success formula is aim, ready, and then fire. The first step in the breakthrough cycle may therefore be the cessation of random activity to allow for focused planning, preparation, and pursuit of a new strategy.

The goal of any breakthrough exercise is to initiate a new success cycle. The key ingredients for that success cycle are the following:

1. A highly articulated and architected strategy that delivers powerful customer and competitive advantages in the market place
2. An organization that is aligned and committed to the breakthrough strategy
3. Structured, systematic, massive and speedy execution of the game plan

The aim, ready, fire framework focuses on delivering these three key ingredients in support of a breakthrough strategy. It may not matter how a company delivers these three essential elements, and certainly conditions and contingencies vary from company to company, but best practices in each of these areas can assist aspiring companies in the pursuit of their outrageous objectives. Most firms go through a success cycle only once; therefore, this is one area where it is particularly wise to look to other organizations for lessons that can help make the process more efficient and effective. On reflection, here are some key generalizations from the experience of these breakthrough companies.

AIM

Much can be said about the aim process, but three key points deserve our attention. *First, and second, the process begins with collective inaction.* The first step can be summed up as, "Don't just do something, sit there!" Cease non-essential activity and focus on core strategy issues for a period of time. The second step involves sitting there together. Securing the focused attention of a senior team on a common challenge is no small achievement. It may take some time to focus the minds of the senior team on the aim process. Participants in the process will undoubtedly conclude that they have more important and pressing things to do. Local, tactical agendas will threaten the emerging strategy cycle at every turn.

It may take some effort to truly engage the group in the strategy cycle. Surveys of the assumptions and concerns of individual executives, with group processing of conclusions, gaps, and areas to be addressed, can be helpful. Team building and coaching work can also be appropriate and effective. One-on-one meetings with the CEO to engage key executives are invaluable. Somewhere in this process, a fundamental question must be answered: "Can this team come together to shape, launch, and execute an enterprise strategy?" In shaping a collective aim, the work itself can do a great deal to pull a senior team together.

During the aim cycle, it is essential to freeze discretionary activities, especially executive hiring, acquisitions, alliances, and major resource-allocation decisions. Inaction is even more impressive and powerful when the organization is facing an impending crisis. Soon enough, extraordinary, focused energy will be unleashed, and the action factor within the organization will rise dramatically. Certainly the new action will be much more precise, synchronized, and powerful.

The aim phase presents an opportunity to collect, synthesize, and focus market knowledge and self-knowledge. It provides an opportunity to think, to debate, and to explore scenarios and options. It needs both first-rate analytical work and the best business acumen to generate, screen, and develop strategy options, elements, and linkages.

The third key point about the aim phase concerns the deliverable. Whatever process is used, the outcome of the process must be a single, integrated strategy, with specific, actionable initiatives, supported by the unwavering commitment of the senior team. That's the only essential deliverable of the aim phase. The key words here are *single, integrated, actionable,* and *commitment,* but if I had to pick one word it would be *focus.* One of the core concepts in Japanese strategic planning is *hoshin kanri.* Japanese firms using this approach devote a great deal of time and energy on the front end of a planning cycle to identify a critical strategic imperative, or hoshin. The ruling principle holds that a company can implement no more than two or three critical programs—preferably one—in any two- or three-year period. After those critical programs are identified, management dedicates most of its time, energy, and resources to ensuring that the hoshin is achieved. The hoshin becomes the object of obsession for the entire firm. Similarly, breakthrough companies focus on a single crucial initiative. Progressive's passion was to provide fast and friendly claims service; Countrywide's was to give quick and inexpensive mortgage approval; American Standard's obsession was to reduce working capital through increased inventory turns. Caterpillar aimed to create a 21st-century manufacturing system. In each case, a sharply targeted program took root across the firm in a disciplined way. Core initiatives took precedence over other priorities within the enterprise and were implemented across functional areas, product divisions, and geographical locations. They enjoyed intense top-down momentum from strong, zealous leaders.

The new strategy often (but not always) includes a specific, engineered value proposition, a tightly defined target market, and other explicit strategy elements. Formal screens may be applied to determine whether the strategy meets acceptable competitive feasibility, resource realities, financial justification, and implementation risk standards. I would recommend this extra work during the aim phase because it should improve the quality of the strategy, reduce risk, and accelerate the time line. Nonetheless many of the breakthrough companies we observed did not utilize a full-scale strategy process or format. Many used pilots and limited launches to test, validate, and refine their breakthrough strategies before making a complete commitment to the new plan. After they were convinced of the potential and power of the new model, they moved aggressively to implement the new strategy.

Here's why a highly developed aim is so important: Breakthrough strategies are all about bold action, but that bold action must be informed, planned, and scripted. One of the firms in our initial sample was Enron. Their transformation from natural gas pipelines to energy trading was a profound and powerful breakthrough. We signed on as consultants in the mid 1990s to work on a follow-up breakthrough to enter the consumer utilities market with a new business model. After just two meetings, we resigned. I must confess it was not because we detected a lack of morality or integrity. What we did detect was a cowboy culture incapable of inaction. Decisions were made without due consideration or process. They were not willing to do the hard work of crafting a grounded strategy before firing their six-shooters. Bold breakthroughs work best when they are launched after painstaking, systematic strategy work. The first step is to perfect your aim as a team. Figure 7.1 shows some of the key elements of the aim phase.

Figure 7.1
The Start of the Success Cycle:
The AIM Phase

Test Assumptions	Accumulate and Analyze the Data	Set Aspiration	Articulate Core Initiatives and Projects
Assay Opportunities	Apply Business Acumen	Describe AIM (Preferred Future State)	Define Architecture of Preferred Future State
Self-assessment			

Align the Senior Leadership Team
→

READY

"A winning general creates the conditions of victory before beginning the war. A losing general begins the war before knowing how to win it."

—*Sun Tzu,* The Art of War

The work of bonding a senior team around a core transformation agenda is the seminal step in implementation. Success in this phase can overcome most other obstacles along the way, assuming the breakthrough strategy itself is sound. The odds of achieving both are improved by engaging senior leaders in depth in the seminal strategy formulation process. In one of our client organizations, we took ten of the top twenty executives off line and sequestered them for six weeks to focus full time on radically redefining the company's vision and strategy. Similar commitments of senior management time are seen in many breakthrough companies.

After the strategy is set and the senior team aligned, it is time to begin preparing the rest of the organization. Don't launch the program until it is very tightly defined and a critical mass of resources of all kinds is in place to support implementation. Premature activation of the program is to be avoided. First, resources for managing implementation must be established, including definition and assignment of senior leadership roles; support staff, communications, training programs, and coaching capacity; and program and project management infrastructure. After these key elements are secure, announce the program with fanfare. A coordinated kickoff will capture the organization's attention and convey important and perhaps novel signals. Show the senior team's commitment and resolve. In organizations with some history of abortive initiatives, coordination, critical mass, and consistency are even more important.

Leadership's message might focus first on conveying the nature and logic of the new corporate vision. Engaging the organization in the new aim is essential, and all available tools and mechanisms should be used to convey a single consistent message. That message says, "We are changing, here is why, here is what we are aiming to achieve, here is how we plan to do it, and here is your role and our expectations." Cascading communication models that deliver presentations to employee groups in person can work well to make the message personal, while mass media prepare the way. Such rollouts may involve extensive group training and communication activities. American Standard sent 37,000 people through DFT training sessions, in 7 languages, in 18 months. At Ford Motor Company, more than 60,000 employees went through small group sessions led by executives to introduce and explain the Ford 2000 strategy.

The ready phase includes more than communication and training. A big part of the ready phase involves freeing up implementation resources and capacity by curtailing low-return, redundant, and obsolete activities and projects. A formal audit of current projects may be helpful in identifying candidates for termination, postponement, or integration. This may also be a good time to review and rationalize product lines, processes, activities, reports, and meetings. The goal is to free up resources that can be redeployed to focus on high-priority projects. Remember that the breakthrough strategy will be delivered primarily by a relatively small group of people whose personal activity portfolios will be strained to the maximum. Anything that can be done to lighten the load for that group of people in particular will provide positive acceleration to the realization of breakthrough. Support for that core group of implementers is essential, and the best thing you can do for them is to reduce the number of demands and distractions they experience.

Redeployment may also apply to human resources. The ready phase may provide an opportunity to replace head count with new talent and capability. Especially in this austere age, many leaders adopt a zero-sum policy about head count, insisting that any additions must be matched by terminations. Lightening the ship can be quite energizing, especially in companies that have not taken a serious look at poor performers, their product and service portfolio, reporting requirements, e-mail, meetings, and management activities. Taking the bottom 10 percent off of any or all of the aforementioned items can create considerable capacity and energy for execution of the enterprise strategy.

During this phase, if it has not yet been done, project teams must develop specific project plans for key enterprise initiatives. In my experience, adequate project management capability and capacity will not yet exist and must be established, and training in project management will be required. It will also be valuable to create and engage a pool of employees to populate enterprise projects on special assignment.

The HR group will have its work to do in designing and delivering training, recruiting new personnel, managing communications, and reworking the performance management system to support the new strategy. At American Standard, for example, the old incentive system was scrapped with the introduction of their DFT initiative. It was replaced by a single incentive—every time total inventory declined by $50 million, the company wrote checks to more than 1,000 employees.

Assignments are a key element of the ready phase. Staffing project teams is a central focus, and senior executive roles as sponsors or customers for projects must also be specified. Remember that most break-

Figure 7.2
Preparing to Launch:
The READY Phase

Align the Organization	Set Key Assignments	Resource Allocation: Deliver Project Resources,	Accountability
Communicate Action Plan	Use A List - Assign Emerging Leaders on Project Teams	plus Program Management Group, IT and Organizational Capacity and Competency	Incorporate Program Targets into Performance Management System
Add-On's – Incorporate Inputs from the Field to Refine Strategies		Prune Existing Activity	Use Personal Contracting

Prepare the Organization
⟶

through programs involve dozens of projects that must be defined, staffed, approved, funded, coordinated, and managed. A program office (or equivalent) is essential. With the aid of the senior leadership council, the program office will identify and fill key assignments and monitor, support, and ensure performance. Assignments must be accompanied by account-ability and resource allocation. Visibility in itself helps ensure success, but sponsors and the senior council will need to be active during the fire phase. Figure 7.2 shows key elements of the ready phase.

FIRE

All efforts to aim and ready the organization will be in vain without successful execution. It's not easy. Transformation is the most difficult task in management. There may never be a better implementer of en-terprise-wide initiatives in a large organization than Jack Welch. During the 1990s, after a decade of organizational preparation and condition-ing and at the peak of Welch's powers, GE executed two enterprise initiatives: Workout and Six Sigma. Neither initiative was truly trans-formational. Neither could be called a full-scale strategy. Both methodologies had been perfected elsewhere decades earlier. The point is that you will need everything you have and then some to execute breakthrough enterprise strategies containing dozens of individual projects that must be linked and coordinated within the master plan. Two key tools can help address this challenge—prioritization and program management.

Prioritization

The typical organization has an extensive portfolio of existing and pending projects, many of which are fundamentally disconnected from the enterprise's core strategy—*if it has one*. A diverse portfolio of projects will overwhelm the firm's scarce implementation resources, resulting in gridlock, even in some of the best companies. I once worked with a midsized health insurer that was trying to address fundamental changes in its marketplace. This firm's operating plan had 132 projects for the coming year. I asked its leaders to reduce the number of operating initiatives to a short list of truly crucial projects. The response was, "You don't understand. This is the short list of critical projects. We worked very hard to get it down to 132 initiatives."

I persisted, requesting the senior executive team to sort the 132 projects into three categories: (1) critical, (2) important, and (3) valuable. At the end of the exercise, we found no projects in category 3 and only three projects in category 2! Not giving up, I asked the five senior executives to list the top 50 projects in order of priority, which they did. We then asked the operating management committee one layer down to rankorder the same 50 projects. The project ranked first by the senior executive team was ranked 47th by the operating group; the senior team's second-highest priority project was ranked 44th by the operating group, and so on. These two important management groups in one firm exhibited an almost perfect inversion of priorities.

Imagine what it was like to be a midlevel executive in this enterprise. Hundreds of projects bump around in various stages of implementation. Project owners scramble for help to complete their efforts. No clear statement of priorities exists to help sort through the many conflicting demands on time and resources. The situation is reflected most visibly in extreme pressures on key bottleneck functions like information systems, where managers end up making critical decisions about what projects ultimately will receive attention. How are these decisions made? Often, locally, based on criteria like the following:

- Which will be easiest?
- Which project owner do I like the most?
- Which project owner is most powerful?
- Which do I think is most important?
- Which does my boss think is most important?
- What's the quid pro quo?
- Which project has the quickest payback?
- Which do my people want to work on?
- Which is most visible?
- Who is making the most noise?
- I think I'll do a little bit on each project.

Resource gatekeepers in each bottleneck area set their own priorities based on considerations like these. Unfortunately, the priorities set at each gate will differ. Because these projects are like series circuits, nothing happens until all the gates are closed. The net result?—Many partially completed projects hang around the resource gateways, clamoring for attention. Gatekeepers, overwhelmed by project overload, become demoralized, paralyzed, or worse. In many organizations, gatekeepers are looking at literally hundreds of initiatives that require their support, with more coming in all the time. I have seen organizations where the number of new projects coming in the gate exceeds outbound completed projects by a factor of 10 or more. Key resource gateways become Bermuda triangles of lost, drifting, and sunk projects. Overload is magnified in companies with highly decentralized operations and autonomous strategies. Managers and teams throughout the firm independently develop large numbers of projects and initiatives. On a stand-alone basis, most of these projects appear to make sense, but the result may be a huge number of unrelated, unconnected, stand-alone project efforts, which quickly deplete the enterprise's precious implementation resources, resulting in execution gridlock.

There is only one answer to this problem. Calculate your execution capacity, increase it where you can, and introduce a prioritization process that queues up and knocks down key projects in an orderly fashion. Be sure that every implementation resource understands the priority system and operates accordingly.

A key philosophical question underlies the prioritization process as the master plan is converted into projects for execution. Should we tackle some small, bite-sized projects with limited scope first to get on the board, or should we focus on the big, critical components of the strategy? Many breakthrough companies clearly prefer to focus on the big, difficult projects first, which—if they are successful—change everything. This approach is highly consistent with the core concept of breakthrough—a nonincremental advance into new territory. If the difficult components can be mastered first, it will pull the organization and the market forward into the future at a much faster rate than will incremental advances. On this front, breakthrough companies are bold, preferring the big bet, especially if the aim and ready work have been done.

These big bets, like ADP's master database, Royal Bank of Canada's Single Reference File (SRF) platform, TRW Credit's Copernicus project, or Progressive's PACMAN system, among many examples, often carry large price tags and require the complete attention of a large part of the organization. To ensure effective execution, professional program and project management becomes essential.

Program Management

Program and project management (PPM) are an increasingly important component of modern business. Once seen primarily of value for engineering and IT activities or in industries like aerospace and construction, PPM is moving into the mainstream. For breakthrough enterprise strategies, a program management office plays several critical roles. It will establish a process for structuring, staffing, starting, supporting, and securing completed projects as prioritized by the senior team. Second, the program management group will develop and deliver best practices and tools for project management and train project managers. Third, it will coordinate and synchronize a large number of projects with staggered start and completion time lines. It will also monitor progress, report to senior leaders, and actively intervene as needed to insure progress. With the right program and project management capability and capacity, execution can become a somewhat systematic exercise. To ensure that the program and project managers do not become yet another source of conflicting demand on organizational capacity, it should be headed by the CEO or COO. Conflicts with day-to-day demands of the business won't go away, but clear signals and priorities can eliminate much of the normal chaos and deliver successful execution of the projects that will drive breakthrough. Program and project management are essential in the fire phase (see Figure 7.3).

TEN TACTICAL TIPS

Here are a series of generic recommendations that represent best practices from successful breakthrough companies.

Figure 7.3
Realizing Breakthrough:
The FIRE Phase

Activation	Administration	Achievement	Attack Breakdowns	Explore Adjacencies
Formal Program Launch	Manage Multiple Projects and Initiatives	Reward and Recognition for Accomplishments	Identify Stalls and Saboteurs, and Intervene as Appropriate	Examine New Opportunities Exposed by Breakthrough
First Wave of Enterprise Projects	Monitor Progress and Manage People Resources	Communicate Program Results		Redefine the AIM
	Program and Project Management	Build Momentum and Confidence		

Value Delivery
➡️

Form a Strategic Leadership Council

It is imperative to engage the senior team in the strategy cycle from the beginning. Determine the membership for this group based on the realities of your organization, including preferably more than five and fewer than 20 top executives. They must be convinced of a compelling need or opportunity to reformulate the company's core strategy. Engage these senior leaders in selecting and articulating the strategy and in the readiness and implementation phase. Unless this senior team is truly committed to a breakthrough strategy, the chances of starting a new success cycle are minimal. The strategy leadership council should meet on one or more extended retreats and as often as needed to develop and maintain team focus and alignment.

Create a SOPO

A second key element in any breakthrough program is the strategy office and program office (SOPO) function. This group provides key staff support to the strategy leadership council in shaping the strategy and plays a key role in program management after the strategy has been architected. The strategy office also facilitates meetings and collaborations between functional and business units and provides the disciplined program and project management support necessary to expedite execution of the strategy. This SOPO represents an excellent opportunity to engage emerging leaders in the organization, although the group should be headed by a member of the senior council.

Use Consultants Selectively

View consultants the same way as acquisitions. Engaging a consultant or making an acquisition is not a strategy, but using consultants or acquisitions to fill in key components of a larger strategy makes all the sense in the world. Both content and process experts can provide critical assistance in support of the breakthrough cycle. Use facilitators to head key meetings, to coach and mentor senior executives, and to bring process expertise to the strategy cycle. Content specialists can also be extremely valuable in helping to shed light on opportunities and threats. Used wisely, they can be superb investments.

Remove Nonstarters from Your Team

Focus on reforming your starting lineup if necessary. For members of the team who are not engaged and committed to the process, much less the strategy, it will be best to part ways sooner rather than later. Many executives agonize over these kinds of decisions, and it can cost an organization years in starting a new strategy cycle. Be straightforward and state simply, "This is what we are going to do and if you cannot be an integral part of this exercise, now would be a good time to depart." There are two fundamental statements here. First, we are going to play as a team, and second, we are going to pick our sport and our strategy together. If these principles are a problem for members of your organization, surface these issues and deal with them sooner rather than later.

Use Personal Contracting

Many of the most effective senior leaders seem to use some version of personal contracting. These leaders set expectations about deliverables in one-on-one conversations outside of any formal budgeting or performance management process. These conversations continue over time and in periodic one-on-one interactions. The topic focus of the dialogue remains constant, and the consequences of success and failure are clear. Personal engagement with peers is particularly powerful, but watch what happens when you develop personal contracts with emerging leaders.

Redesign the Performance Management System

For breakthrough strategies to be successful, key target objectives, metrics, and milestones must be incorporated into the formal performance management system. Reward and recognition must be tightly coupled to the new strategy. Should compensation continue to be calculated primarily as a function of traditional operating results, the gap between running today's business and creating tomorrow's business may become insurmountable.

Communicate Extensively

Many senior leaders in my experience complain that they have communicated their vision exhaustively, yet no one seems to get it. There is no limit to the power of communication. Be sure communications are consistent and continuous. Plan on delivering the same message hundreds of times in hundreds of settings with different media. Use the new power of the corporate Intranet for communication and deployment of the strategy. When you have become completely tired of the topic, the organization is beginning to get it.

Aim High, Deliver Now

Hockey sticks are not a necessary part of the breakthrough cycle. Breakthrough is not about making heavy front-end investments to secure returns in the distant future. Program deliverables should be sequenced to ensure realization of results in the near term. UTi adopted a rule that limited all projects to a maximum duration of six months. Larger projects were broken into value release stages to ensure that results would be harvested in a timely fashion.

The concept of the Power of AND from *Built to Last* shines through in all breakthrough companies.[3] It is possible to deliver growing and improved current performance while building foundations for breakthrough. It is possible to be the low-cost leader and deliver superior customer service. It is possible to show rising revenue growth rates with increased margins and profits. It is possible to do today's job and create the future at same time. A big part of the Power of AND comes from focus and prioritization, and part of it also comes from new processes and technologies, but fundamentally it is a state of mind.

Develop a Corps of Enterprise Leaders

Breakthrough strategies provide a wonderful opportunity for emerging leaders to demonstrate their capability. Invite their contributions and recognize their achievements. The creation of a formal corps of emerging leaders can provide a pool of resources to be used in staffing key projects and initiatives. Many of these special assignments may be stretched on top of existing responsibilities, whereas others may be full time in nature. Your next-generation business model provides a powerful vehicle for bringing out your next generation of leadership.

The Leadership Factor

The final key element in the success cycle is the senior leader's role. This single factor outweighs all the other elements in importance and is the subject of the final chapter. The senior leader acts as the owner and architect of the breakthrough cycle. He or she must define and drive the aim, ready, fire process to bring out the best in his or her organization.

NOTES

1. Transforming Globally-Integrated Manufacturing, MESA Research Report, May 1993.

2. op.cit.

3. James C. Collins and Jerry I. Porras, *Built to Last,* Harper Business (New York), 1994.

CHAPTER 8

THE LEADERSHIP FACTOR

ANY TEAM, with the right leadership, can achieve outrageous objectives. The question really is not so much the quality of the individuals in the team; rather, it is their ability to work together as a team. The larger and more important question, however, is the following: Does senior leadership have the characteristics and qualities essential to ensure success? Here are questions to help you determine whether your leadership has what it takes.

- Can you make the painstaking effort to develop a highly articulated master plan for your strategy?
- Can you align the senior team to fully support that strategy?
- Can you stay focused on and committed to the same core strategic program for a minimum of three to five years? For the rest of your career?
- Can you give the same speech hundreds of times?
- Can you establish and manage 50 to 100 personal contracts

with key executives who will deliver the key components of the
strategy?

- Will you intervene when necessary to remove roadblocks and obstacles to breakthrough?
- Would you if necessary remove your closest colleagues from their
positions if they became the principal barrier to successful execution of the breakthrough strategy?
- Can you balance day-to-day demands and distractions with your
commitment to the breakthrough program?
- Can you ensure that the financial and organizational resources
necessary to deliver breakthrough will be available as needed?
- Will you and your team monitor every gate in every series circuit
in the organization to identify and address breakdowns?

If you can stomach all these questions, you have what it takes to launch
and execute a breakthrough strategy. Not all leaders and organizations
have the ability and capacity to turn breakthrough strategies into reality.
There is really no point in developing a radical strategy if successful execution is unrealistic. Think before you leap. Self-assessment begins at the
top. Does senior leadership have the qualities necessary to drive the shaping and execution of a breakthrough strategy in your organization?

The first item on the list is *personal capacity*. Breakthrough CEOs universally exhibit extraordinary capacity—for strategic and operating detail and for managing extensive personal networks; although these may be
qualities common to senior leaders in general, breakthrough leaders dis-
tinguish themselves from their peers in this area. These leaders grasp the
details. A related success factor is in-depth operating experience. Deep,
granular knowledge of how the business works provides an invaluable
edge in shaping and executing radical strategies. A surprising number of
the CEOs in this study literally grew up in family businesses as second-
or third-generation leaders. They knew every facet and every face of

their business and used that knowledge to great advantage in shaping and staffing their strategies.

Great breakthrough leaders are *multitalented*. The best professional analogues for a breakthrough leader may be architects and general contractors. The best leaders possess the systematic, structural design skills of the architect and the organization and execution skills of sophisticated general contractors. But both analogues only represent part of the CEO's role. Breakthrough leaders do much more. They play the combined role of general manager, coach, and quarterback of a professional football team.

Breakthrough leaders are heroic. The fundamental quality shines through in all the leaders we observed, and it is reflected in their pursuit of great accomplishments and victories. This quality is intimately tied to a second aspect of personality. In *Good to Great,* James Collins describes humility as a core quality for successful senior leaders.[1] My favorite reference on this subject is an observation about mountain climbers by Robert Pirsig: "To the untrained eye, the difference between an ego-climber and a selfless climber is not readily apparent."[2]

Pirsig concludes that ego-climbers, those climbing the mountain solely for self-aggrandizement, don't make it to the top. The analogy to leadership is clear and appealing. Much of the research on executive derailment would support this view.[3] However, the fact is that ego-climbers make it to the top of many organizations. Far too many jobs are held by men and women who are there primarily for their own enrichment and glorification. Selfless leaders are all too rare. We found wonderful examples to fit the profile of the selfless leader, but humility was not a common attribute of the breakthrough leaders we observed. Strong egos were more prevalent than selflessness. Yet, strong ego need not mean weak integrity, and ego may be part of the hero's psyche. Mainstream thought in venture capital circles seems to view ego as a positive quality in venture leaders. In my experience, humility is not essential to effective CEO leadership. Several failures we tracked were led by selfless, dedicated, hardworking

CEOs of great humility and integrity, while visiting some of the successes seemed like an exercise in ego-tourism. Yet, if I were to pick one CEO who best captures the essence of breakthrough leadership, humility stands out as a core quality.

My choice for best breakthrough leader would be Mano Kampouris of American Standard. Although I stand in awe of many breakthrough leaders, Mr. Kampouris, who would correct me for addressing him that formally, sets the standard to which others should aspire. Emanuel (Mano) Kampouris was born in Egypt and educated in England. He began his career in Europe and moved up the ladder within American Standard to the post of Executive Vice President by 1990. When American Standard took itself private in a management buyout, Mano's peers elected him to head the new company. Although he holds the title of Chairman and CEO, Mano's business card reads simply, "Group Leader."

Mano's honeymoon was brief, as a recession in the early 1990s shrank U.S. housing starts to the lowest levels since World War II, and American Standard's business dropped dramatically. Meanwhile, failure to meet debt service obligations would mean handing over the ownership of the company to the lenders. The stakes were high. The company had to find the cash to service the debt. It sold all noncore assets to raise cash but still came up short.

In funding the leveraged buyout, American Standard had converted its pension plan into an ESOP, so every employee's retirement was at stake. Searching for sources of cash, Kampouris began to focus on the company's billion-dollar inventory position, and study teams were formed to search for ways to improve working capital efficiency. A Colorado consulting company offered a promising solution to reduce working capital levels and improve cash flow. American Standard tried this demand flow technique at its Tyler, Texas plant, and it worked. At a meeting of the senior management team, Kampouris told the group, "Without significant change, we will lose the company." He asked everyone on the senior team to "sign in blood" to support implementation of the DFT initiative. The outrageous objective was zero working capital, and the first step on the path to that goal was twice net turns or TNT, a program to double inventory turns in less than two years. That initiative was launched immediately and aggressively. Mano took his "100 best people" and put them on a mission to convert DFT methodology into new processes for American Standard. The result, called FastTrack, was rolled out soon thereafter across the organization. A massive training effort was launched in seven languages at more than 100 plants in 34 countries. Participants were tested to ensure proficiency, and each plant was given its own DFT targets.

The core of DFT involves a build-to-order or "pull" production system that can manufacture and ship units the same day of an order. Pull systems require extreme labor flexibility, as production schedules are determined in real time. Yet, American Standard is a highly unionized company, with thousands of electrical workers, pipe fitters, machinists, and other traditional union employees in its plants. A typical U.S. plant contained 35 specific union craft categories. Transformation at American Standard involved converting these individual union crafts into four supercrafts. Employees were trained and compensated to add additional craft capabilities, increasing flexibility within their facilities. Excess employees were converted into coaches, and downtime was used for training. Coaches were assigned for everyone in the organization. A Center of Excellence for coaching was established to train and monitor coaches as they worked with fellow employees on development of new skills and implementation of DFT. *American Standard executed its transformation in record time with virtually no employee turnover.* American Standard achieved annual productivity growth of about 7 percent in the 1990s decade. Growth absorbed the excess labor.

In Kampouris' words,

> Breakthrough requires total and unequivocal commitment from the CEO. You can't flinch once. You have to give it one hundred one percent or it will never work. We gave DFT top priority over every-

thing. You have to be passionate, relentless, and constant in your focus on the big goal. Twenty percent of your employees will think that the program is a joke, that it's a cosmetic effort, and one or two bad apples can kill the whole thing. You can't let that happen.

Watching Mano in action, I was struck by his tireless focus on key tasks. In addition to unrelenting focus and sheer physical stamina, his management style is characterized by a powerful combination of *humanism* and *directiveness.* Mano epitomizes a successful hands-on management model. Frequent visits to factories around the world focused on local progress to date, with constant comparisons to sister facilities. Meetings with other American Standard executives were never complete without a detailed review of DFT progress and status. For the better part of the 1990s, Kampouris spent the bulk of his time in hands-on management of the DFT program. A hardworking, principled, and high-performing executive, Kampouris sets a standard that makes his peers pale in comparison.

Now Chairman Emeritus, Mano is tackling a new outrageous objective. Kampouris is focusing his considerable energy on helping to stimulate a moral revolution in the mainstream of American corporate leadership and society.

Let us reflect for a moment on the question of heroism and humility. One of the most intriguing historical perspectives on breakthrough innovation can be seen in this quote from Thucydides, in describing the Athenians of the Golden Age:

> They are addicted to innovation, and their designs are characterized by swiftness both in conception and execution. They are adventurous beyond their power, daring beyond their judgement, and sanguine when in danger.

I can think of no better description of bold breakthrough leadership. Yet Athens would be a poor role model for a breakthough organization. Athens' glory lasted only one lifetime. The Golden Age commenced following the sack of the city by the Persians in 490 B.C. and ended before the Spartans reduced the city again in 404 B.C. It was an extraordinary success cycle but blazingly brief! Wracked by internal dissent and crippled by misadventures in Sicily and the Dardenelles, Athens fell to their more focused and disciplined Spartan rivals. The Spartan commander Lysander is attributed to have said, "Boldness is an affront to the Gods. It breeds Hubris, and Hubris calls forth Nemesis. Nemesis brings Hubris low."[4]

Is it possible to be simultaneously bold and humble? To be innovative and grounded? Mano Kampouris embodies that uncommon combination of qualities. The best breakthrough leaders are grounded visionaries. A Greek without hubris and a deeply religious man, Mano described his outrageous objectives in the following fashion: "We selected a goal we could not achieve on our own. We set an impossible goal that could only be achieved with God's help."

FAILURE FACTORS

If senior leadership deserves the bulk of the credit for successful breakthroughs, they must also answer for failures. The single most deadly—and unfortunately quite common—failure factor we encountered was an inability to align core members of the senior team around a common strategy. Although lack of alignment is usually manifested in polite noncommitment and noncompliance with core strategies, it often appears in a more direct fashion. Many companies clearly operate as weak confederations of very powerful local fiefdoms who focus on their own local agendas and priorities. That model may work well for a conglomerate, although that presumes the individual businesses have the leadership qualities and resources to initiate and manage their own success cycles. The confederate corporation will not thrive in most settings. Yet, a surprising number of CEOs seem unable to enlist their colleagues' commitment to or command their compliance with enterprise strategies: Leadership begins here.

A second common failure factor revolves around hands-on ownership and management of the strategy. Successful breakthrough leaders surprised me by the extent to which they were engaged in the details of strategy formulation and implementation. They were in constant touch with the front lines of the breakthrough effort. Many senior leaders are more detached and aloof from the details, and they may exhibit a tendency to delegate ownership to lesser leaders. One of the most unfortunate failures in our study involved Levi Strauss and Company. Levi Strauss was one of the most spectacular early success stories we saw. With the introduction of its LeviLink system, Levi Strauss pioneered a series of new supply-chain, logistics, and retailing innovations that only now are becoming mainstream practices. The early results with LeviLink, which introduced the use of bar code tags on apparel items for inventory management purposes, were spectacular. In the early 1990s, retailers using the LeviLink system were able to dramatically reduce stock-outs and markdowns and were able to increase their volumes and margins significantly. The benefits to Levi Strauss were even more significant. In attempting to scale up this initiative to redefine core processes within Levi Strauss, leadership for the initiative was given to the company's CIO, and great reliance was placed on external consultants in the design and implementation phase. Both steps raise red flags. I believe the lack of true involvement and commitment from senior leadership was the key reason for Levi Strauss's failure to fully capitalize on its LeviLink breakthrough.

The third category of failure is somewhat more subtle. A significant number of the companies in our sample were acquired during or after their breakthrough. In many of these cases, the momentum of the breakthrough was curtailed following the acquisition. US West, which possessed one of the best senior management teams we encountered and an extraordinary leader in the person of Sol Trujillo, was beginning to achieve significant traction in its new customer service and marketing initiatives when it was acquired by Qwest Communications. Literally all of US West's talented top team departed following the merger, leaving the company in questionable hands. The result was a disaster, bringing a promising telecommunications concern to its knees. New leadership is now attempting to restart the cycle at Qwest.

Selling out can look very attractive when compared to the very hard work of implementing a breakthrough. Often, however, the potential for breakthrough is lost on sale of the company, especially if there is a transition in leadership. Certainly the sale of the firm may signal a financial success—but not a strategic success. For most breakthrough leaders, financial success alone would not be sufficient.

Failure can also stem from poor strategy, and strategy is ultimately the responsibility of the CEO. The best way to avoid poor strategy is to hold your fire until you have perfected your aim. But what if the scene changes? It's likely that the scenario will have already been considered in the strategy process, and the strategy can be adapted as conditions change.

The most common strategy shortcoming is a failure to support high aspirations with a grounded master plan. Outrageous objectives cannot be realized without a meaningful performance or profile breakthrough. Any grand goal—especially those of a financial nature—are pipe dreams without grounded performance and profile innovations that convert into growth, improved margins, and enhanced market position. One way to overcome this problem is to define the outrageous objective in primary terms—that is, in terms of operating metrics or profile milestones themselves. Financial or competitive position goals in themselves are not enough.

A critical hazard in any breakthrough strategy is separation of the future strategy from today's business and organization. Every effort must be made to integrate the two. A related failure factor is long lead times on deliverables for the breakthrough strategy. If lead times are too far out, the tendency to separate the breakthrough strategy from day-to-day life will be magnified. The breakthrough strategy should be broken up into discrete deliverables with focus on near-term results. At UTi, Roger MacFarlane insisted on quarterly value releases for the NextLeap effort. NextLeap incorporated a theme called "Twenty to the Power of Five." Five targets were specified, including an increase in net operating margins from 10 percent to 20 percent over five years. This target was reduced to quarterly and annual goals, and key projects were delivered each quarter. Monthly and quarterly management reports highlighted the progress and deliverables in the NextLeap effort. CEO Bill Zollars of Yellow Corporation put it more simply: "You put a light on the distant hill and then watch the ground in front of you."

Roger MacFarlane and his colleagues at UTi also made every effort to incorporate NextLeap into line management's day-to-day attention. A new incentive system was introduced for line executives, which was calculated on current performance, plus adjustment for success or failure in meeting key NextLeap targets. Revision of the reward or performance management system is an essential ingredient in implementation of any breakthrough strategy. That single step can neutralize the universal tendency to separate strategy implementation from daily activities and priorities.

The failure factor to be most feared is the absence of credible commitment from senior leaders. Any organization will probe and test its leaders for any sign of wavering commitment to core programs. I once met a woman named Rose who was responsible for a small but important part of a billing system in a telecommunications company. Rose would frequently be asked to assist with different projects within that organization. She put it the following way: "I can smell whether this is a serious project or not, and I can tell almost instantly. I can tell whether the project leader is committed or not. If it doesn't smell right, I'm not going to put any time and effort into it." Every organization has many people like Rose. Their natural skepticism may be well justified. It's imperative the Rose and others like her see and feel the sincerity of commitment to projects so that they can make their own contributions. These contributions must be earned, honored, and reinforced every day.

ADVICE FOR ASPIRING LEADERS

The best breakthrough leaders exhibit a series of common qualities, attributes, and approaches. Here are some of the key characteristics that I would highlight as part of the ideal management style for a successful breakthrough leader.

Be Hands-on

The best breakthrough leaders are intimately involved in the inner workings of their programs. They know who is responsible for each piece of the program and where it stands. The mere fact that the CEO is informed of progress—or the lack of it—gives an incredible impetus to implementation. Communicate and demonstrate that knowledge on a daily basis and get involved in the details; often this may simply be a physical presence and a few informed comments and questions. Other times it may be more of a cheerleading or morale-raising role, in other cases it may involve intervention in the event of a breakdown, and certainly it should involve personal, face-to-face recognition for key contributors. At US West, CEO Sol Trujillo was a tireless worker. It was not uncommon for his executives to receive phone calls late at night or early in the morning with comments or questions from Sol on something he just read or reviewed. He kept current on almost everything going on in the organization and stayed in touch with those driving key pieces of the company's programs. Don't overdelegate.

Leave No Doubt

In debriefing successful breakthrough CEOs, one of the most common remarks sounded something like the following: "If I were to do this over, I would proceed with much greater confidence and certainty." There is a time at the front end of the strategy cycle when an open mind and access to numerous options are particularly valuable, but as the strategy cycle proceeds, it is critical that the CEO project an air of great certainty and confidence in the chosen path. This is more than acting. Confidence and certainty results in concise decision-making, aggressive resource allocation and a very high "action factor." One of Mano Kampouris's goals was to increase the ratio of productive time to elapsed time within his organization. After the DFT program was set, he implemented a program to reduce meetings across the country by 70 percent. Certainly, there remained needs for coordination and collaboration, but the need for great discussion and lengthy decision processes was eliminated. To paraphrase an old joke, "the meetings will continue until morale improves." As soon as your strategy is set, stop pussyfooting around and get on with it!

Set High Standards

Although a bold breakthrough goal can be reduced to manageable chunks, the implementation will inevitably stretch your organization's capacity to its limits. It is important to recognize that breakthrough will require a significant personal sacrifice for many employees and executives. At the same time, for many, the breakthrough will be the best period of personal and professional growth and satisfaction in their careers. This will be a time that will demand the most from everyone in the organization; that should be the standard expectation, and the key corps of leaders who are will contribute the most to the breakthrough effort must be supported, recognized, and motivated to meet extremely high standards. These principles apply first and foremost to senior leaders. Prepare yourself for a period of extraordinary effort. The breakthrough cycle will test your stamina. It is fundamentally a marathon race, and you must be conditioned and prepared for that type of grueling effort. At the same time, it is the leaders that will set the pace for the group of runners. Plan on running five-minute miles.

Engage Personal Partners

The breakthrough cycle provides a unique opportunity for a set of leaders to come together and accomplish something significant as a team. It provides a window for personal bonding, and many breakthrough CEOs seem particularly skilled at building these bonds. A number of successful leaders relied heavily on one or two key partners. John Gaulding of ADP, perhaps the most scientific of the breakthrough CEOs we studied, had a very close relationship with his alter ego, COO Gerhardt Blendstrup. Another great example of a strong CEO/COO combination can be seen at Progressive Insurance, where Peter Lewis, a highly innovative CEO, relied heavily on COO Bruce Marlow in implementation of their immediate response system. A combination of an engaged CEO with complete control of the big picture and a hardworking COO on top of every detail is a powerful one. Perhaps surprisingly, the COO position is a vanishing species. That position has become a victim of divisional organization models emphasizing senior division heads who report directly to the CEO. Even in many single-line businesses, the COO is not present. In some cases, such as Mano Kampouris of American Standard, the CEO actively embraced and performed the role of the COO as well. Although he was able to manage both roles, a strong team of two executives would seem to be a superior solution.

Another key piece of the leadership equation may well be a program management office or the equivalent. In companies where there is a COO, that can become part of the COO's role, and that one person can then best integrate the enterprise projects with the demands of day-to-day operations. In the absence of a COO, the program management head is even more critical, although he or she will find it more difficult to move the program forward in the face of day-to-day demands without active senior executive support.

The HR leadership role is also key in transformation programs. In a surprising number of breakthroughs, no senior HR leadership was present in the organization, and those functions were performed by other senior executives. In other cases, senior leadership was frustrated in the ability of senior HR leaders to perform as part of a strategy council when formulating and implementing a breakthrough strategy. It is clearly a gap for many companies, and it is also clear that a strong strategic HR leader is an invaluable asset in the transformation process. Savvy HR leaders working as partners shoulder to shoulder with line executives can contribute immensely to the success of any strategy cycle.

Reward and Recognize

I believe it is imperative that the company's reward and performance management system be reconfigured to focus rewards around the achievement of key milestones in the breakthrough strategy. Without that change, momentum for the new strategy will ultimately wither. Personal recognition is also a key component of this equation. In a number of our consulting engagements, I have requested that one hour per week of the CEO's time be filled with personal phone calls to individuals deserving of recognition for their contributions and achievements. Those phone calls are great morale builders for both parties (they may also be used as reminders or remonstrations). Many successful leaders devote considerable personal time and energy to formal reward and recognition activity.

Make it Mainstream

There is a tendency for breakthrough programs to become a spectator sport. Many of these programs are planned and deployed from the center of the organization, and many members of the company could become passive participants in the program. One way to limit this tendency is to build frameworks to incorporate local contributions and initiatives into the program. Mechanisms for identifying, rewarding, and sharing local achievements are an important part of this effort. More fundamentally, local implementation of the programs deployed from the center will ultimately determine the success or failure of the strategy. At UTi, the central corporate goal of establishing 20 primary logistics partner (PLP) relationships with key global customers is one of the key targets of NextLeap. In addition, each of the company's 200-plus branches were asked to identify their key candidates for local PLP status, and programs were designed and deployed to target, engage, and grow those candidate customers. Local adoption and use of new systems, processes, and services was also a key focal point, and these targets were incorporated into the performance management and compensation system.

Deal with Dissent

Breakthrough leaders were universally concerned with this issue. All of them recognized that a percentage of their employees would be skeptical or worse in response to the new strategies. Passive resistance was one thing, but active dissent and sabotage were quite another. John Gaulding had this to say: "One dedicated saboteur can undo the work of hundreds of committed change makers." Of all the leaders we examined, Gaulding was the most aggressive in repopulating his organization. Where American Standard implemented their transformation in less than three years with 10 percent turnover, Gaulding's group had a turnover of about 80 percent. Al Shulman, CEO of Ecolabs, described it this way: "I don't want any dissent from the field. They are soldiers. Their job is to execute our strategy." They may not be politically correct, but such approaches can be quite successful, assuming the strategy is the right one. Make every effort to engage and align the organization, and be prepared to deal with those who will not participate in the program.

Be Repetitive

Remember that most members of the organization are not there yet. I remember speaking to Mano Kampouris about five years into the DFT program. Mano said, "If we stay with this for another couple of years, it will finally start to be embedded in the foundations of this organization." Keep a singular focus, convey a consistent message, reinforce positive momentum, and cut off distractions.

Create Structure and Process

Successful implementation can be accelerated dramatically through a formal management model. Create a group of specialists whose sole job is to support the delivery of the breakthrough strategy. Create program and project management capability and use standard processes for identifying, defining, staffing, launching, and delivering enterprise projects. Make that a core competency of your organization, and tie that process tightly to your strategy leadership council. This capability will not only ensure progress towards your strategic goals, but it will also give you a surprising level of agility in the near term should new realities emerge. Look to your IT organization for tools and processes that can be extended to more general use. Odds are that they already have expertise in architectures, project management, prioritization systems, and more. Also, strong communications capability is invaluable in any breakthrough effort. Be sure to have a skilled communications leader on the core team.

Be Humanistic and Directive

The best breakthrough leaders exhibit a combination of high humanism and high directiveness. Command and control leaders, who do not lack in directiveness, often come up short on human touch. We have seen breakthrough leaders use this traditional style with effectiveness, however. Directiveness is an essential ingredient in the breakthrough equation. High executive and employee turnover, however, are also part of that equation. Many of the firms we studied exhibited extremely high turnover rates during the breakthrough cycle. Some of the companies we would cite as benchmark success stories fall into this category, including ADP's ACS group and Progressive Insurance, for example.

Those leaders who combine humanism and directiveness, so long as they deal with dissent and distraction, seem to be able to engage and inspire their organizations to accelerate the breakthrough cycle. American Standard, which epitomizes this approach, was able to implement its breakthrough program in two years, whereas Caterpillar, with a very similar program, experienced significant labor difficulties that delayed the implementation of their breakthrough program by several years in contrast. American Standard's investments in coaching and training and its humanistic leadership style paid big dividends in accelerating breakthrough results. Lou Gerstner at IBM, who also epitomizes the combination of high humanism and directive leadership, stands out as another example of swift and successful execution of a breakthrough strategy. IBM's long-standing commitment to respect for the individual and heavy investment in human capital development were central to the success of their extraordinary transformation. I conclude that directiveness is an essential component of breakthrough leadership, and humanism is a significant accelerator of breakthrough.

One of the most frustrating failures we encountered occurred at Ford Motor Company. I found Jac Nasser to be a superb breakthrough leader. Like Mano Kampouris, he was born in the Near East and worked his way through Ford's international division before being appointed CEO of Ford in the mid-1990s. Jac Nasser possessed extraordinary in-depth knowledge of Ford's operations and a passion for automobiles. He created an ambitious vision for Ford and converted it into a set of key enterprise initiatives designed to modernize and globalize Ford's operations. The program was designed with great detail and precision. Considerable effort was made to communicate with, prepare, and train the organization, and numerous high-priority projects were launched with the right kind of staffing, resources, and senior support. In my experience at Ford, a large number of executives in this awakening organization were on fire with passion for this program, and significant results were being delivered to redefine and globalize core operations, introduce new products, and renew the Ford brand. At the same time, Nasser implemented a performance culture program designed after GE's model, which called for forced performance rankings and mandatory retirement for the bottom 10 percent of the organization. Ford's traditional culture viewed the transformation effort as too harsh in its handling of people. An "us and them" schism began to appear in the organization. Ultimately, the cultural and organizational trauma associated with Nasser's program created a backlash that led to his replacement, and transformation at Ford has slowed to a crawl. It is likely that a more humanistic approach might have yielded better results.

The Greater Good

It is a great privilege to be around great people, especially if you can join them early in their journey. One rather remarkable leader I had the good fortune to work with is Christel de Haan, cofounder of Resort Condominiums International (RCI), a highly innovative company that created the market for trading vacation timeshares. Christel immigrated to the United States as a teenager and went to work initially as a secretary. As cofounder of RCI, she remembers all too well the years in which the fledgling company moved forward on fumes alone. Convinced of its greater potential, Christel bought out her partner and became sole owner and CEO of RCI. She developed a vision of RCI as market champion of a large and growing industry. She invested heavily in advanced technology and systems to support growth and market leadership. In working with Christel during this phase of the company's growth, I was struck not only by her engaging energy and humility, but by her sheer hard work and stamina. Many evenings at 9:00 p.m. or later, Christel would announce, "Hey guys, it's after 9:00, should we go to dinner or should we keep working?" She would ask the question in all sincerity. Fortunately, most evenings we were able to persuade her not to go back to the office after dinner, but the senior team at RCI spent a large number of early mornings, long days, and late nights together as they crafted and executed RCI's strategy. By the late 1990s, RCI achieved annual profits in the $200 million range. When RCI was acquired by Cendant Corporation, Christel began to focus her energies on a new initiative, creating a network of hubs to provide educational, medical, psychiatric, and other services to orphanages and orphans in third-world countries. Today, there are dozens of Christel House hubs around the world providing services to many thousands of orphans whose lives will be materially changed because of Christel de Haan's vision and compassion.

Foreign-born and without a formal education, Christel de Haan became perhaps the most successful female executive/entrepreneur of her generation. She aimed high, worked hard, and motivated her team, as did all successful breakthrough leaders. What really distinguishes her leadership approach was the unique, genuine care she demonstrated for her employees and executives and for the extended industry community her company led and served. *Great leaders focus on the greater good.*

Senior leaders are in a natural position to see the best interests of the entire enterprise. They can best put local priorities in perspective. They can best see possibilities for collaboration and collective action. Focus on the greater good is an essential characteristic of the best breakthrough leaders, and it is a quality that will be increasingly important for emerging leaders in most organizations. Cultivate that focus and make it central in all decision making.

Let us now ask a larger question: Is focus on the greater good of the corporation subject to the same criticism as a division leader's obsession with local priorities? Are senior leaders repeating the mistake of division leaders who fail to see the larger picture and focus on their own local priorities at the expense of the enterprise? *The best breakthrough leaders think even more broadly.* Certainly they focus on the well-being of customers. Peter Lewis of Progressive described how a $30 million investment decision was made: "We didn't really look at the financial justification for this investment. We felt it was something we had to do for our customers." John Goulding at ADP was clearly focused on bringing benefits to all the participants in the extended auto insurance sector. Christel de Haan at RCI cared intensely about the well-being of the extended vacation time-share industry and treated all participants in the industry as if they were members of her own family. The best breakthrough leaders think not only of all of their immediate stakeholders but also of the well-being of their extended business community.

But even focusing on the extended industry can be justified in financial terms. Many breakthrough firms and leaders make commitments to an even larger community. Target Corporation is a pioneer in its commitment to community service, contributing 5 percent of net profits to community betterment. Target's outrageous objective of becoming the best company in the world contains five specific goals. Target aims to become the best in the world in four of those categories, and it intends to remain the best in the world at community involvement and betterment.

It is perhaps notable that leaders like Mano Kampouris and Christel de Haan, now retired from their corporate leadership positions, are dedicating themselves to social service. Tiger Wessels, chairman of UTi Worldwide, takes as much pride in his company's contributions to black empowerment and education in South Africa as in its business accomplishments. Concern for and commitment to the greater good are core qualities of the best breakthrough leaders.

NOTES

1. Jim Collins, *Good To Great,* Harper Business (New York), 2002.

2. Robert Pirsig, *Zen and the Art of Motorcycle Maintenance,* Corgi Books (London), 1974, p. 206

3. See Morgan W. McCall and Michael M. Lombardo, *Off the Track: Why and How Successful Executives Get Derailed,* Center for Creative Leadership, Technical Report No. 21.

4. Steve Pressfield, *The Tides of War,* Doubleday (New York), 2000, p. 479.

APPENDIX I

BREAKTHROUGH PROFILES

Breakthrough Organization	*Core Strategy*
ADP (ACS Division)	ACS revolutionized auto repair claims management with its comprehensive data base, estimation tools, mobile computing, body shop management systems, and electronic parts network.
Amazon Inc.	First significant e-tail company, market leader in book sales, expanding to broad general merchandise line.
American Airlines (Sabre)	One of the first firms to realize the potential of information services, Sabre also developed a leading position in web-based travel services through its Travelocity unit and was spun out in a 1996 IPO, valued in excess of $5 billion.

Breakthrough Organization	Core Strategy
American Standard	Implemented DFT globally, quadrupling inventory turns, cutting cycle times by 90 percent, improving quality and reducing costs. Completely restructured antiquated, unionized factories to best-in-class performance.
Barclays Bank (UK)	Barclays pioneered personalized banking through aggregation of customer information and the creation of enterprise infrastructure to support integrated service offerings.
BC Systems Corp (Canada)	Now a Canadian Crown Corporation, BCS pioneered online services in the public sector, dramatically lowering costs and improving customer service.
Blue Cross Blue Shield of Missouri	Missouri Blue pioneered online medical support services with its Health Care Xchange system.
Cable and Wireless Ltd.	C and W developed best-in-class business customer service and billing systems, reflected in the highest rates of customer retention in the industry. It is now working to establish itself as a leader in business Internet services.
Caterpillar	Implemented its PWAF Program to cut cycle times by 90 percent, reduce defects and cut warranty payments by 40 percent, cut factory floor space while increasing capacity, more than double the number of products offered, and create a new business unit, Caterpillar Logistics.

Breakthrough Organization	Core Strategy
CR England	This trucking company introduced its MBI system to significantly increase fleet capacity, safety, and on-time performance; and establish electronic links to customers for enhanced service and cost reduction.
Charles Schwab	Discount stock broker broke out of its niche by perfecting Internet-based stock trading and financial services.
Countrywide Credit	Upstart home loan originator revolutionized its industry by integrating loan processing functions into a single job—the Loan Committee of One—using core process integration and innovation, advanced technology, and job redesign to cut cycle times by 90 percent and transaction costs by 80 percent while improving customer service. Total loans issued grew from $2 billion to $50 billion in 3 years as CCR captured market leadership in home loans.
Daiei	Running neck and neck with Wal-Mart as the world's largest retailer, Daiei pioneered retail credit cards, financial services, and diversified services for consumers.
Dassault Systemes	This French aerospace company became the market leader in CAD/CAM tools and systems.

Breakthrough Organization	Core Strategy
Dell Computers	Dell perfected a breakthrough strategy that uses JIT supply techniques, direct sales channels, and mass customization to seize leadership in PCs.
EMC Corporation	EMC has achieved a breakthrough hat trick by first redefining competitive standards in network storage, by introducing open storage systems, and by migrating to storage area networks.
France Telecom (Minitel)	Minitel, as the first public online services network, provided a preview of the power of the Internet.
IBM Corporation	IBM's transformation into services and solutions, with leadership in e-commerce, revitalized Big Blue.
Intermountain Health Care	This pioneering health care provider created the HELP system to support informationalized medical care.
InfoCalifornia	An early public sector program designed to use online services to improve health, welfare, and employment offerings to end-users.
JC Penney	JC Penney has quietly established itself as the largest catalog and direct marketing company in the United States.
Levi Strauss	The LeviLink system pioneered the use of bar codes and EDI in apparel retailing to drive inventory management gains and supply chain efficiencies. Attempts to redefine core processes around the new approach foundered.

Breakthrough Organization	*Core Strategy*
Logan Aluminum	Logan's Technical Application System combined real-time monitoring of hundreds of data points in their production system with statistical process control to significantly improve quality standards in the aluminum industry. It also set new standards in product precision and supply chain integration.
MANCO	This impressive little company pioneered the use of activity-based costing by channel, customer, and transaction to shrink S, G, and A overhead expense to 11 percent of sales, prior to its acquisition.
Mervyn's	Mervyn's significantly improved operating performance and profitability through a breakthrough program to redefine purchasing and merchandising processes.
Micro J	This small company was a leader in introducing online recruitment systems with its packaged recruitment management system and database.
Motorola	Motorola launched an aggressive effort to capture leadership in wireless web services.
Mrs. Field's Cookies	This cookie-baker commercialized its retail operations management system, ROI, through Fields Software Group.

Breakthrough Organization	Core Strategy
New Brunswick Tel (now Aliant Corp.)	This provincial telephone company is the world's most advanced, leading the way in the provision of integrated electronic services and charting the future of electronic living.
Nortel	Nortel successfully made the transition from analog to digital switches and is a leader in integrating traditional telephony, IP technology, and optics.
Phillips Petroleum	Phillips Business Information System captured and delivered real-time inventory, price, and volume data for petrochemicals to field decision-makers, doubling ROI in one year.
Plains Cotton Cooperative	Still a little-known company, PCC created the world's first electronic market, revolutionizing the cotton industry, and now is the largest market for cotton trading in the United States.
Premier Professional Services	Spin-off from S. C. Johnson and Sons Company brought new levels of sophistication to HR management systems.
Progressive Insurance	Innovative insurance company radically reduced claims settlement cycle times, cutting costs and improving customer service, and leveraged its lead into rapid growth in auto insurance.
RCI Corporation	Created and dominated the market for time-share trading prior to its acquisition by Cendant Corporation.

Breakthrough Organization	Core Strategy
Royal Bank of Canada	RBC, today widely considered the most technology-advanced bank in the world, launched its SRF system to unify all customer data and support customer service and development initiatives, as a forerunner of current business intelligence systems.
Rosenbluth Travel	This tiny travel agent created a $5 billion business by integrating multiple airline computer reservation systems into an informationalized platform for outsourced corporate travel management.
Seagate	This resilient disk drive maker wins the award for continuous innovation and sustained market leadership through its agile R&D, rapid ramp, transition management, and quality control competencies.
Southwest Airlines	Southwest's operational and human resource innovations have led it from subregional status to market champion in air travel.
Sun Microsystems	We worked closely with Sun in setting up e-commerce capability for its supply unit in the early to mid 1990s. That breakthrough program was an early and significant success, but it was only part of this pioneer's transformation into a core player in the Internet revolution.

Breakthrough Organization	Core Strategy
Times–Mirrors Books	Times–Mirrors' textbook group introduced a series of breakthroughs, including digital production techniques, custom textbooks, online services, and more, before its acquisition by McGraw-Hill.
Toyota Motors	The Toyota manufacturing system, with its core principles of lean manufacturing, JIT supply, Kaizen continuous improvement, and design for manufacturability underlies Toyota's continuing success and its expansion into new areas such as prefab housing and aircraft.
TRW Corporation	TRW Information Services grew into a $1 billion information services business before its acquisition by Experian.
Toto Corporation	Japan's leader supplier of bathroom fixtures is morphing into the world of smart toilets and "acquagenics."
USAA	This insurance provider implemented an integrated enterprise information platform and core processes to support its strategy of expanding offerings to core customers.
US West	One of the original regional Bell companies, US West made rapid progress in implementing bundled, broadband consumer services prior to its merger with Qwest.

Breakthrough Organization	Core Strategy
UTi Worldwide	This fledgling freight forwarder built a global network and is expanding rapidly into integrated logistics partnerships.
Veteran's Hospitals	We were surprised to discover that the Veteran's Hospital Administration was the most innovative health care network in the United States. The VHA has implemented innovative client care initiatives to proactively address problems common to its customer base, and it shares best practices within its redesigned and focused hospital network.
Vons	A leader in the development and application of advanced technology and processes in retailing, Vons' breakthrough led to its acquisition by Safeway in 1996.
Wal-Mart	This storied retailer continues to define the state-of-the-art in procurement and supply chain efficiency through new vendor-managed inventory and distribution initiatives.

Appendix II

BREAKTHROUGH COMPANY STOCK PRICE PERFORMANCE

Company	Share Price As of July 1				% Gain		
	2003	2002	1998	1993	1Yr	5Yr	10Yr
ADP	34.29	42.21	36.94	12.13	-18.76	-7.17	182.7
Amazon[1]	37.25	13.55	19.02	N/A	174.9	95.85	N/A
American Standard	74.03	74.93	45.00	N/A	-1.20	64.51	N/A
Caterpillar	54.74	48.00	53.94	18.50	14.04	1.48	195.9
Charles Schwab	10.39	11.00	7.72	1.38	-5.54	34.59	652.9
Countrywide	69.85	48.86	52.31	20.17	42.96	33.53	246.3
Dassault Systems[2]	32.38	44.50	48.88	15.5	-27.24	-33.76	108.9
Dell	31.92	25.18	23.48	0.29	26.77	35.95	10907.0
EMC	10.56	7.08	10.96	1.32	49.15	-3.65	700.0
France Telecom	24.54	11.23	71.25	34.6	118.5	-65.56	-40.99
IBM	83.59	67.60	58.38	34.6	23.65	43.18	141.6
JC Penney	16.62	20.86	71.25	12.31	-20.33	-76.67	-35.0
Motorola	9.57	14.3	17.64	13.94	-33.08	-45.75	-31.35
Nortel	2.9	1.47	14.02	3.31	97.28	-79.32	-12.39

Progressive Ins.	73.96	57.22	51.25	10.29	28.91	43.92	616.8
Qualcomm	36.04	26.43	7.02	3.74	36.36	413.4	863.6
Royal Bank[3]	42.71	34.46	30.59	11.62	23.94	39.62	267.5
Sabre[4]	24.99	24.05	37.19	31.62	3.90	−32.8	−20.97
Seagate	19.5	11.25	N/A	N/A	73.33	N/A	N/A
Southwest	17.13	15.43	8.96	5.83	11.02	91.18	193.8
Sun Microsystems	4.79	4.72	5.37	.92	1.48	−10.8	420.7
Target	37.62	36.75	25.00	4.13	2.36	50.48	810.9
Toyota	52.23	52.00	52.44	29.38	0.44	−0.4	77.77
UTi Worldwide	31.33	20.10	2.40	N/A	55.87	1205.4	N/A
Wells Fargo	50.71	49.33	38.56	13.49	2.79	38.56	275.9
Wal-Mart	54.35	54.40	30.25	12.68	−0.09	79.67	328.6
Breakthrough Company Average					26.21	104.67	765.9
Dow Jones (DJIA)	9040.95	9109.79	9048.67	3510.53	−0.756	−0.085	157.5
NASDAQ Composite	1641.77	1403.8	1914.6	703.58	16.95	−14.25	133.3

Sources: Annual Reports, NASDAQ.com.

[1] Earliest trade date is May 15, 1997.
[2] Earliest trade date is June 28, 1996.
[3] Earliest trade date is October 16, 1995.
[4] Earliest trade date is October 11, 1996.

POST FACE

In a project of this magnitude, the list of people owed a debt of gratitude is extensive. I would first like to thank Al Barnes of IBM's Advanced Business Institute, the cofounder of the original research project. Al provided invaluable support along the way. Bob Howe, then head of IBM Consulting and later CEO of Scient, and Ginni Rometty of IBM Global Services, among many other IBM executives, provided key support to the project along the way. The research team included a number of MESA Research employees, many of whom were former students from USC's Marshall School of Business. Key contributors were Chuck Leatherbury, who did yeoman work at a number of the early research sites; David Flores; Chris Lee; Sandy Hom; Chris Noblet; Brian Himot; and my partners Ron Hubert and Eric Anderson. Wendy Owen managed and delivered the preparation of the final manuscript. All these individuals' contributions are greatly appreciated. The core contributions to this book, however, came from the many executives who shared their experiences with us. To those executives at each of the companies in our sample who participated in this study, our gratitude is great. In addition to those companies and executives mentioned in the book, special thanks go out to Sol Trojillo, John Kelly, and Sue Parks of US West; Julie Shimer of Motorola, now CEO of Vocera; Bill Zollars, Greg Reid, Don Barger, and the senior team at Yellow Corporation; Barry Leskin of ChevronTexaco, Jim Wright of Motorola, Bill Gaik and Brad Branch of Deloitte & Touche, John Whalen and colleagues at BAE; and Steve Kerr of USC, GE, and now Goldman Sachs.

I would also like to thank several key thought leaders who had considerable influence on my own development, particularly Ray Vernon, my mentor at Harvard Business School who showed me how to balance the real world of business and economics with the thoughtful world of academics in a powerful manner; Ted Levitt of Harvard Business School who embodies the spirit of that great institution on the Charles River; Michael Porter, who with his own breakthroughs renewed the field of corporate strategy; Jag Sheth of Emory University; Brian Quinn of Dartmouth's Tuck School; Warren Bennis of USC; James Collins; and Gary Hamel. Each have made extraordinary contributions in the world of strategy and leadership, and it is my outrageous objective to join their esteemed company.

INDEX